AMERICAN
MARKETING
ASSOCIATION

MARKETING

TOOLBOX

Developing Successful Marketing Strategies

David Parmerlee

NTC Business Books
a division of *NTC Publishing Group* • Lincolnwood, Illinois USA

This book is dedicated to every young child
with learning disabilities.

Library of Congress Cataloging-in-Publication Data

Parmerlee, David.
    AMA marketing toolbox. Developing successful marketing strategies/
  David Parmerlee.
      p. cm.
    Includes index.
    1. Marketing—Management—Data processing. I. Title.
HF5415. 13.P3245 1992
658.8'00285—dc20

                            92-14242
                              CIP

Published in conjunction with the American Marketing Association
250 South Wacker Drive, Chicago, Illinois, 60606.
Published by NTC Business Books, a division of NTC Publishing Group
4255 West Touhy Avenue, Lincolnwood (Chicago), Illinois 60646-1975, U.S.A.
©1993 by NTC Business Books. All rights reserved.
No part of this book may be reproduced, stored in a retrieval system, or transmitted in any
form or by any means, electronic, mechanical, photocopying, recording, or otherwise,
without the prior permission of NTC Publishing Group.
Manufactured in the United States of America.
2 3 4 5 6 7 8 9 0 VP 9 8 7 6 5 4 3 2 1

AMA Marketing Toolbox

Many marketing management books define marketing and provide terminology definitions. The *AMA Marketing Toolbox* has a different purpose. This series will guide you in collecting, analyzing, and articulating marketing data. Although there is some narrative that describes the components of marketing processes, these books define the relationships between the processes and explain how they all work together. The books also supply formats (or templates) to help you create sophisticated marketing documents from your data.

A SYSTEMATIC PROCESS . . .

Because markets change constantly and new marketing techniques appear all the time, a step-by-step system is needed to ensure accuracy. These books are process-based to allow you to be as thorough as possible in your marketing activities and document preparation.

. . . FOR PROFESSIONALS

Although these books are written with a "how-to" theme, they are written for marketers who have experience and who know marketing terminology and the objectives of the business function of marketing. The *AMA Marketing Toolbox* consists of the following books:

- *Identifying the Right Markets*

- *Selecting the Right Products and Services*

- *Evaluating Marketing Strengths and Weaknesses*

- *Developing Successful Marketing Strategies*

- *Preparing the Marketing Plan*

ROLE OF MARKETING STRATEGIES

How do marketing strategies you will formulate in this book fit in with other market planning processes? Marketing strategies in this book are based on three basic levels of marketing—strategic, departmental, and functional—and the three disciplines of marketing—research, analysis, and planning. This structure allows you to develop marketing strategies that are tailored to any size company with any product or service.

The books in the *AMA Marketing Toolbox* series will help you go from data collection, to analysis, to planning and control, and eventually to implementation of marketing plans. The diagram below indicates where the books fit into this process.

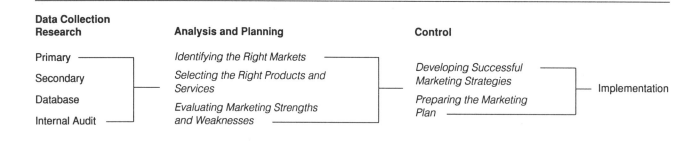

Data Collection
Research

Primary

Secondary

Database

Internal Audit

Analysis and Planning

Identifying the Right Markets

Selecting the Right Products and Services

Evaluating Marketing Strengths and Weaknesses

Control

Developing Successful Marketing Strategies

Preparing the Marketing Plan

Implementation

ABOUT THE AUTHOR

David Parmerlee is a marketing analyst and planner who works with selected clients. He is past Vice President of the Marketing Management Services Group at American Marketmetrics, Inc. A marketer with more than 12 years of experience, his approach has a financial orientation rather than the more traditional communications approach. His background is in secondary and audit research with a focus on process-based planning and implementation.

Parmerlee has worked for several major corporations, including Anheuser-Busch, Pitney Bowes, and Arthur Young (now Ernst & Young). He has represented clients in industrial, consumer, and service-based markets and has written articles for regional and national publications. He is a member of the Direct Marketing Association and the American Marketing Association, where he serves on the board of directors and the national board of standards for professional development and certification.

Parmerlee received his degrees in marketing and advertising from Ball State University in Muncie, Indiana. He is also certified as a consultant specializing in training and ethics.

Contents

Part 2 / Data Reporting: Formats   77

Introduction

WHAT IS A STRATEGIC MARKETING PLAN?

What is the difference between a strategic marketing plan (SMP) and a marketing plan (MP)? An SMP is an attempt to analyze your current situation, identify the needs, problems, and opportunities facing your company (from a marketing perspective), define your marketing goals and objectives, and then develop marketing strategies to meet these goals. The MP extracts the SMP data and strategies and applies them on a one-year timetable. The MP is the final action plan; the SMP is foremost a process. The SMP is a three-to-five-year strategy, out of which is born the annual MP.

Although the SMP covers all levels of marketing management, the SMP primarily deals with the strategic corporate and business unit levels, while the MP deals more with the departmental and functional levels. The SMP establishes how the business of marketing will be conducted in your specific marketing situation. SMP does this by defining operational policies, practices, and procedures. The SMP is also highly financially oriented in regards to your products and marketing efforts.

People often ask, "what is marketing?" Once, the answer would have been a simple one-sentence conceptual description based on marketing activities. This book defines marketing in terms of structure, as illustrated in Exhibit 1. This structure is based on the basic levels of marketing— the strategic, departmental, and functional levels (which will be explained in later sections) and the three basic disciplines of marketing—research, analysis, and planning.

Exhibit 1
The Structural Model of Marketing

	Strategic	Departmental	Functional
Research			
Analysis			
Planning			

The structural model of marketing demonstrates marketing's multiple capabilities. The biggest confusion of the non-marketing community is differentiating marketing as a whole from the nine functional components, such as sales, advertising, or distribution, and from its corporate-level strategic components. Business often views just one of these marketing components as all there is to marketing. However, marketing can be broken down into two interrelated attributes: function and business structure. Another confusion comes from separating marketing management research concerning product, market, and marketing activities from marketing research at the functional level, such as media, sales promotion, and customer satisfaction research.

This book will use the terms *marketing mix* or *marketing functions components* interchangeably to indicate the many activities that constitute marketing as a whole.

WHY CREATE A STRATEGIC MARKETING PLAN?

The purpose of a strategic marketing plan is to identify needs, problems, and opportunities that can impact your financial "bottom-line." You assess ways to save money by becoming more efficient in your marketing activities and ways to make more money by uncovering new options in your product line or market. To do this, you must isolate three basic elements of marketing—the market, the product, and the management of marketing activities, at the strategic, departmental, and functional marketing management levels.

The strategic marketing plan establishes who you are, whom you serve, what you offer them, where you are today, where you want to be tomorrow, and when and how you get from here to there.

You must be as objective as possible in establishing your current marketing situation and in developing your strategies. If you analyze only part of your marketing situation (e.g., your product), or if you focus your marketing strategies on only one marketing function (e.g., advertising), you will have a plan that is unbalanced and unrealistic.

HOW DOES THE STRATEGIC MARKETING PLAN RELATE TO OTHER MARKETING PLANNING PROCESSES?

The strategic marketing plan tells a story about your present marketing situation and strategies and explains what, why, how, when, and where events and activities take place, and how you will approach your marketing situation in the future. From the strategic marketing plan you will develop your action or implementation plan to reach your goals.

A strategic marketing plan is similar to a long-term personal financial plan. The first thing you need to do is establish your current financial situation. To do this, you must identify your expenses and sources of revenue. Then you need to analyze your situation to establish needs, problems, and opportunities. Upon completion of that process, you then define your goals and objectives. Next you establish how you are going to obtain your goals. Here you select an action plan that will make your dream a reality. Then you establish a timetable for events and activities. Finally, you need to include a system of control to track and measure your effectiveness at working toward your goals. This will allow you to make adjustments to your plan as needed.

WHAT IF YOU ARE PREPARING A SEPARATE MARKET STRATEGIES ANALYSIS?

Developing marketing strategies, as stated earlier, is usually part of an overall marketing plan. However, if you are presenting marketing strategies as an independent document, it should include the following elements:

1. Title page or cover page
2. Table of contents
3. Executive summary (including the purpose of the analysis and its major findings)
4. Methodology
5. Limitations
6. Marketing strategies (body of report)
7. Exhibits

HOW SHOULD THIS BOOK BE USED?

This book provides you with a set of marketing planning formats to help you prepare a document in which your strategic marketing plan can be presented in an organized fashion. Part 1 demonstrates the use of the formats; Part 2 includes the blank formats themselves.

In using this book, the author strongly suggests you obtain three other books in the AMA Marketing Toolbox series: *Identifying the Right Markets, Selecting the Right Products,* and *Evaluating Your Strengths and Weaknesses.* You can use this book alone, but the series is designed to work together for the most consistent results.

The processes and formats in this book are designed for a consumer market, such as consumer packaged goods or retail service outlets. They can be adapted to your market's needs, problems, and opportunities. Throughout this book, you will be alerted to many possible adjustments you may need to make in the strategic marketing plan. To conserve space, each format shows a limited number of lines for products, whereas your firm may have fewer or many more products to consider.

Note: Units 3 through 6, the action parts of the process, present exercises using the structure shown at right. Remember that there is usually only one strategic and one departmental level, but there are as many as nine functional levels. You may want to break out each functional area when performing each exercise in these units.

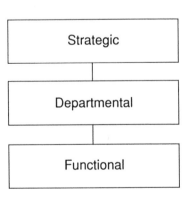

Part 1

Data Analysis

Unit 1

Preparing Your Strategic Marketing Plan

Before you can begin the process of strategic marketing, you must first establish your current marketing situation. In most textbooks, a strategic marketing plan's first component is the situation analysis; its purpose is to establish the present status of all marketing efforts. The series of which this book is the final part modifies the situation analysis as follows. First, you collect the necessary marketing data. Next, you place that data into marketing processing formats using the first three parts of the series:

- Identifying the Right Markets

- Selecting the Right Products

- Evaluating Marketing Strengths and Weaknesses

However, for marketers who do not use the other books in the series, this book is designed to accept various forms of marketing information. The methodology of this book requires only that you organize the information you have acquired into three categories: the marketplace, your product offerings, and your marketing activities. Because this book is designed as part of a strategic planning system, you may need to adjust your research to this book's structure.

The objective of Unit 1 is to help you prepare the data you will need to utilize this book. When you move into Unit 2, Identifying Your Needs, Problems, and Opportunities, you will already have established where you are in your current market, product, and marketing endeavors, and you will be ready to begin translating your data. For the purpose of creating a strategic marketing document, you will also need to prepare a situation analysis, either as an exhibit within the document or as a separate document. It is advisable to read through the entire strategic marketing plan book to understand its approach and the information needed to make the plan operational.

WHAT IS DATA ANALYSIS? Data analysis is reviewing data that have been collected in raw statistical or non-statistical form and then translating what that body of data is saying.

By doing this, you can make a diagnosis and prescribe a programmed strategy to fit the data findings. Unfortunately, in marketing we are not to the point where you can simply input data, push a button, and then output the next marketing move. There are simply too many different market situations. The next best solution is to design a process where you can input raw data in set formats or templates where you can organize and evaluate the data.

The first three books in this series do just this: they provide a structure for you to review and assess your data. With a few exceptions, they don't tell you what to look for or what the data are saying. But they do point out any missing data and provide you with your own reference point to compare with national norms and standards. Whether you use the formats in this series or your own system, the first thing you should do is determine the approach you will follow and the objectives you will pursue.

Why Should You Use Structured Formats?

The purpose of placing your data into a structured format is to be able to uncover data that may represent needs, problems, and opportunities. You need to establish your objectives in collecting the data and then interpret what your results tell you about your current marketing situation.

Your approach to data collection.
First, you should determine how you will go about obtaining the body of information that will form the basis for your analysis and planning activities. Configuring your approach carefully will help get you from point A to point B in a clear and controlled manner.

Expected results.
Although in marketing you should always guard against preformed conclusions, formulating in your own mind what you would like to see materialize is acceptable. You should simply be aware not to prejudge. Instead, you should try to visualize your expectations with this exercise. The bottom line is that you don't want to predict the outcome; you want to prepare for the outcome by identifying what the data reveal regarding the outcome.

What Are Your Process and Methods?

Before you can begin analyzing and organizing your data; you must first perform research activities that will provide you with the data needed to perform this entire planning exercise.

Your research methodology.
The methodology for this series is based on findings obtained through defining the marketplace, your product offerings, and your marketing activities. The following outlines illustrate how the data should be collected, analyzed, and evaluated.

Market research examines the generic structure of a marketplace you are presently in or might wish to enter. The key is that you are collecting data regarding a market you are considering or that currently exists, with little or no interpretation of your own. The following outline reflects the first book in the series, *Identifying the Right Markets*. It shows you what your market analysis data should include.

   I. Market Identification

      A. Market Definition (Mass or Segmented)

      B. Market Size

      C. Market Penetration

      D. Market Factors

      E. Marketing Mix Industry Standards

      F. Secondary Target Markets

  II. Customer Profile

      A. Customer Identification

      B. Reasons for Purchases

 III. Competition Analysis

      A. Identification

      B. Measuring Strengths and Weaknesses

      C. Evaluating Marketing Strategies

 IV. Regulatory Restrictions

      A. Customer Requirements or Government Regulations

      B. Meeting Requirements

  V. Previous Market Research Results

Product research examines your product's value as it relates directly to your customers. The difference between market research and product research is that in market research you address all components of a market's structure. One of these components, customers, are viewed in market research in terms of their habits and trends of human/buyer behavior. Product research deals primarily with customers' direct responses to your product. This gives you customized information regarding your specific product's performance.

The following outline reflects the second book in this series, *Selecting the Right Products*. It will show you what your product research data should contain.

I. Product Identification

   A. Product Line Definition

   B. Product Profile

   C. Brand Identity Profile

II. Product Management

   A. Product Life Cycle

   B. Product Portfolio Profile

III. Product Performance

   A. Product Sales

   B. Product Sales Patterns

IV. Product Profitability

   A. Product Price/Cost Structure

   B. Product Profit/Revenue Structure

   C. Return on Investment

V. Product Production Capabilities

   A. Product Production Capacity

   B. Resources and Limitations

   C. Operational Control

VI. Product Legal Situation

   A. Copyrights, Patents, and Trade Secrets

   B. Product Liability

   C. Outstanding Legal Issues

VII. Product Research and Development

   A. Activities Past and Present

   B. Stage of Activities

   C. Product Testing and Research

Marketing research and *marketing functional research* examine your internal marketing management capabilities. Marketing research includes all marketing management activities, and marketing functional research includes only the marketing mix components (e.g., advertising media response tracking). For this exercise, you are dealing with your entire marketing department.

The following outline reflects the third book in this series, *Evaluating Marketing Strengths and Weaknesses*. It will show you what your marketing research data should contain.

I. Marketing Management Identification

    A. Sales and Revenue Forecasts

    B. Market Share Assessment

    C. Marketing Organization Evaluation

    D. Marketing Operations Review

    E. Business Expansion Activities Analysis

    F. Marketplace Strategy Assessment

    G. Positioning Strategy Assessment

    H. Penetration Strategy Assessment

II. Marketing Function Activities

    A. Marketing Research

    B. Product Management and Development

    C. Pricing

    D. Distribution

    E. Sales (Management)

    F. Advertising

    G. Promotions

    H. Public Relations

    I. Legal Activities

III. Marketing Function Activities Scheduling

    A. Marketing Activities Timetable

    B. Media Scheduling and Buying

IV. Marketing Budget

    A. Individual Marketing Functions' Expense Reports

    B. Overall Marketing Activities Expense Report

V. Marketing Control Procedures

    A. Monitoring Effectiveness

    B. Updating

These outlines provide you with methods of approaching data collection and formats to use in pouring that data into a well-organized structure to be analyzed.

Locating sources of data.

Depending on the area you are researching (product, market, or marketing), your research methodology will be different. Traditional methods of research focused on using primary research, but there are other methods of research available, such as secondary audit and internal database research.

A consumer market has more sources than an industrial market for obtaining related market data. Appropriate secondary sources include scanner data, syndicated databases, census reports, and reference books. You can also perform direct primary market research or commission consultants to perform it for you.

For product research, only primary research is appropriate, because you are looking for information that pertains to only your products and customers. Your can commission consultants to perform primary product research.

For marketing management and marketing functional research, you have several options. Database and audit research are technically types of secondary research. Database research looks at how you are currently managing and marketing to your current database customers. Audit research provides you with information regarding the management of your marketing operations. You can commission consultants to perform database and audit research.

In the entire *AMA Marketing Toolbox* series, with the exception of the market audit, no research processes are explained. The reason is that in research, every situation is different. As a result, you will have to design your own research structure for your specific needs.

Analysis and Evaluation

After you have collected and organized your data, the next step is to determine what it all means. You do this by analyzing and evaluating the data you have obtained and establishing your present status. Your objective is to establish a baseline from which to measure your progress.

Structuring your data.

As stated earlier, ideal analysis would be to input data into a system that would output your action strategies. However, marketing is inexact; this analysis system simply attempts to view your data and then determine what they are saying. This is done by observing either the actual data obtained or the problems, needs, and opportunities revealed by the data. Then you need to begin evaluating the data's validity and importance. The objective is to assess every detail in the data obtained to determine what they indicate about your current marketing situation.

Results.

Once you have gone through the process of collecting, organizing, analyzing, and evaluating your data to form your situation analysis, you need to determine your results. Earlier you established your expected results, and here you have the actual results. Your goal is to compare the two and establish *reality-based results*. The other reason for determining your actual results is, of course, to prepare you for the next move, which is to translate your present marketing situation into meaningful answers and convert those answers into strategic planning actions.

PREPARING TO ASSESS AND FORMULATE

The following paragraphs are intended to help you link your situation analysis with the remaining components of the strategic marketing plan, whether you have used the other books in this series or your own system.

Translating Data

First, you will translate your organized, qualified data into a format that will allow you to identify needs, problems, and opportunities. This format will provide you with structure in processing and converting your analysis findings into actions. This is done by assessing which parts of your data fit, relative to the strategic marketing plan structure used.

Processing data.

To translate your data, you will first eliminate information that does not pertain to the structure provided in this book. You will simply extract the data you think might answer the questions asked in the needs, problems, and opportunities section.

Converting data.

Once you have identified and extracted the data that will best tell you what you need to assess and formulate your situation analysis and needs, problems, and opportunities, then you need to begin converting that data. You will simply plug the data into the formats provided in Unit 2. In interpreting the data, you will act in the three marketing management levels: strategic, departmental, and functional.

To effectively and thoroughly dissect, identify, and select opportunities, needs, and problems, you need to establish structure for manipulating the translated and processed data. You do this by taking each management level and by viewing how each of the three situation areas work at each level individually and together overall. This conversion exercise will allow you to better understand the methodology of this book and prepare you to be as detailed as possible regarding your strategic marketing situation.

	Levels		
Situation Areas	Strategic	Departmental	Functional
Marketplace Product Offerings Marketing Activities			
Marketplace Product Offerings Marketing Activities			
Marketplace Product Offerings Marketing Activities			

Interfacing with the Overall Process

This book is laid out in a system that is based on three areas: **marketplace, product offerings,** and **marketing activities.** The book also translates these three areas into various levels of marketing management. All three areas must be considered in making the entire system work.

CREATING THE STRATEGIC MARKETING PLAN DOCUMENT

After you have completed the strategic marketing plan process, you are ready to prepare the strategic marketing plan document. To do this, you will use a format that presents your strategic marketing plan to the various marketing departments and to upper management. This document should contain both narrative copy and charts or models so that it is interesting in terms of content and appearance. With every document you prepare, you should include an executive summary. This part of the document gives the reader an overview of what the strategic marketing plan has established.

Preparing the Executive Summary

The executive summary is a one- or two-page summary of your strategic marketing plan, which outlines your current situation, proposed plan, and financial implications as a result of actions. Like your mission statement, it should be brief, clear, and to the point. Whether your company is small or large, your executive summary should never be more than two pages in length; ideally, it will be only one page long. In the strategic marketing plan, it needs to focus on the combined marketing management levels (strategic, departmental, and functional) but especially on the strategic level.

Your current situation should include your three analysis components: product, market, and marketing. You should address all conditions and changes that could affect you. It should also include the needs, problems, and opportunities you have identified as a result of your analysis findings. Your proposed plan should first define your mission, goals, and objectives in response to your current situation. Then it should present strategies and tactics, concentrating on the principal action programs and recommendations. Control should also be mentioned in passing. The final portion is devoted to the financial impact of your plans from the marketing point of view. Items such as revenue generation, marketing cost control, product profitability, and sales volume expectations need to be summarized.

Preparing the Quantitative Support

Once you have presented your summary, you will provide the reader with a quantitative view of your marketing goals and objectives (not forecasts). Format 1 provides an idea of elements you may want to include.

Format 1

Quantitative View of Marketing Goals and Objectives

Marketing Activity	Goals and Objectives	Time Period
Sales/revenue (volume)		
Individual products	*Increase by 10%*	*Annually over next 5 years*
Product line		
Market share (new/repeat customers)		
Holding	*Maintain a share of 50%*	*Each year for the next 5 years*
Gaining		
Profitability		
Price		
Profit margin	*Retain a gross profit margin of 45%*	*Over next 5 years*
Return on investment		
Marketing costs		
Control	*Obtain cost levels of 29% each year of sales*	*Over next 5 years*
Percentage of sales		

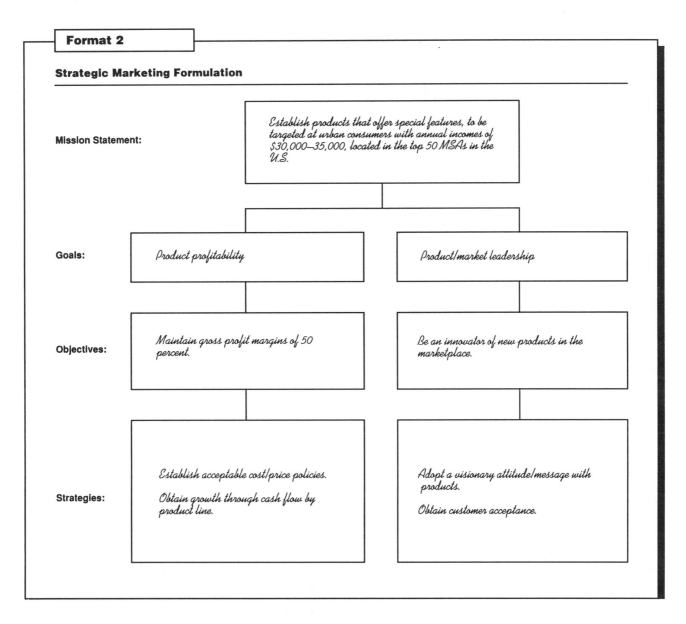

Format 2

Strategic Marketing Formulation

Mission Statement:
Establish products that offer special features, to be targeted at urban consumers with annual incomes of $30,000–35,000, located in the top 50 MSAs in the U.S.

Goals:
Product profitability

Product/market leadership

Objectives:
Maintain gross profit margins of 50 percent.

Be an innovator of new products in the marketplace.

Strategies:
Establish acceptable cost/price policies.

Obtain growth through cash flow by product line.

Adopt a visionary attitude/message with products.

Obtain customer acceptance.

In addition to the quantitative display, you might also want to include a flow chart model of your overall strategic marketing formulation (See Format 2). You can have three separate models for the strategic, departmental, and functional marketing management levels, or you can use the strategic level to represent your entire approach.

SUMMARY Most strategic marketing plans include a situation analysis. To keep this *AMA Marketing Toolbox* flexible, this book offers you instead the option of performing a situation assessment separately, assuming that you can extract the necessary data to be placed in the assessment formats. The bottom line is that you establish where you are today and where you are currently heading, based on your current marketing actions. The purpose of Unit 1 is to prepare you for the strategic marketing plan process.

Unit 2

Identifying Your Needs, Problems, and Opportunities

Once you have established your current situation analysis, you are ready to translate that information into actions. The process of strategic marketing planning begins with assessing your needs, problems, and opportunities. Unit 2 is an interface mechanism to translate the findings established from the various analyses (situation analyses) and to link that data with proposed marketing actions. Before beginning this exercise, you need to recognize a series of terms that will be used throughout this book. This first series of terms defines your situation by determining and assessing three situation elements: **needs, problems,** and **opportunities.** The situation element's role is to provide you with a converter mechanism to take your analysis findings and place those findings into any or all of the three categories.

The next series of terms defines how you will place those categories into a format that allows you to assess what it all means. Each situation is defined by three input areas: the **marketplace,** your **product offerings,** and your **marketing activities.**

The next series of terms acts as a structure that will allow you to apply your situation elements and areas into marketing efforts. This step will help you draw conclusions and establish what will be required of you. Then, provided that you can adjust to your new course of action, you will need to convert this conclusion into action as defined by three marketing management levels: **strategic, departmental,** and **functional.**

The name of the game in this section is subjectively extracting data that you have collected and then subjectively interpreting that data to what they represent and mean.

The final series of terms are the situation element formats: **origin identification** and **strength and weakness measurement.** The situation element formats are presented for the transfer and manipulation of data. The origin format isolates the basis of the situation element. Your goal with this format is to identify the source and the motivation of the situation element. The measurement of strengths and weaknesses isolates the importance of that situation element. This will allow you to determine if the elements are worth pursuing as a company. This format is more difficult to determine, due to the complexity of assessing how strong an element is, how much value it might bring, or how much impact it will have on your company. The key is to try to extract data and apply that data in a manner that will tell you something about your current situation.

For presentation purposes, you will want to include not only your narrative answers, but also the basis for your assessment, including specific documentation and models or charts from your earlier analysis findings.

Exhibit 2-1 displays the entire concept of taking information through a series of stages. These stages act as a funnel with a series of strainers at the end. At the top of the funnel, your objective is to load your original data. Then you sequentially fill and drain, fill and drain, until you obtain a refined substance. You are trying to identify and define, check and verify, isolate and assess elements that may affect your marketing efforts.

Exhibit 2-1
Refining Your Original Data

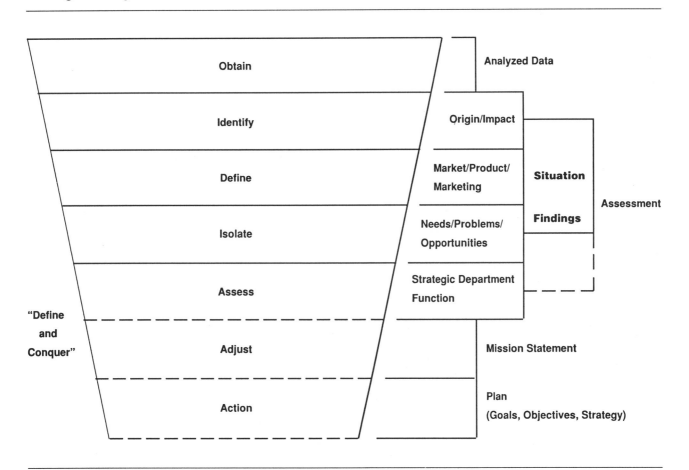

Note: In the following assessment, you will be asked to distinguish between needs, problems, and opportunities. If you have problems determining the difference, don't worry; the purpose of the exercise is not to know the differences among these elements, but to concentrate on the element's impact.

DETERMINING AND ASSESSING YOUR MARKETING SITUATION

The objective of this exercise is to select and extract data found in your various analyses and funnel those findings into your situation assessment. This means you are looking at your situation's elements, areas, and levels and cross-referencing them. By breaking down your findings in this manner, you act as a doctor: examining the patient, making a diagnosis, and selecting a treatment.

Identifying Needs

A *need* is defined as a force, usually positive in nature, in which something necessary or desirable is required or wanted. A need can exist on its own or be created by some entity for someone else. Your goal is to identify the situation's needs and then establish how to meet those needs. Then you must assess what that need means to you in terms of value, and how it might impact your marketing actions positively or negatively. In identifying a situation's needs, you should divide your situation into the three situation areas: marketplace, product offerings, and marketing activities.

Remember that in addressing the issue of need, as a marketer you are interested not only in the need itself and its origin, but also how that need translates to a need for your company to meet.

Marketplace needs.
When addressing needs that arise from the market itself, you are primarily looking at the customer element of the market structure. Usually a customer need exists because customers are not being satisfied by either current products offered by the competition and your company, or alternatives. There is also the situation where customers are very satisfied with current selections, but a company is able to create a new need, such as Miller Lite beer in the early 1970s. Format 3 addresses the origin of market needs, and Format 4 addresses their strength.

Your objective is to assess whether there is a need for some product or service in your marketplace. Your source for data will be your market analysis findings. Your goal is to determine whether the need is worth pursuing. Remember, in assessing the market's needs, you are primarily concerned with patterns and trends of previous, present, and future customers.

Product offerings needs.
Another place where needs exist is in the products themselves, specifically your own products. In addressing the marketplace needs, you are looking at existing conditions within the market structure. In addressing product needs, you are looking at your previous, present, and future offerings that may produce a need. This type of need comes from customers and their needs directly associated with your product offerings. Format 5 addresses the origin of product needs, and Format 6 addresses their strength.

Your objective is to determine what type of needs customers may have—with your products only. You will need to add, modify, or delete

Format 3

Origin of Market Needs

Need Type	Basis of Need			
	Customer	Competition	Regulatory/Environmental	Other
Willingness to pay money for product	*Yes*	*Yes—Alternatives*		

Format 4

Strength of Market Needs

Need Type and Cause	How long has it existed?	How strong is it?	How valuable is it?	What is its impact?
Willingness to pay money —selection of alternatives	*Forever*	*Very strong*	*It governs the decision to purchase.*	*It can slow down sales in both volume and frequency.*

Format 5

Origin of Product Needs

Need Type	Basis of Need		
	Product Feature	Product Benefit	Other
Product's ability to meet customer needs (ABC produced)	*Yes*		

Format 6

Strength of Product Needs

Need Type and Cause	How long has it existed?	How strong is it?	How valuable is it?	What is its impact?
Meeting customer needs —changing habits	*Last 5 years*	*Sales dropped off 30% over last 5 years as a direct result.*	*If product modifications are not made, product must be deleted.*	*Cornerstone product to overall lines; if it goes something needs to take its place.*

Format 7

Origin of Marketing Activities Needs

Need Type	Basis of Need			
	External	Internal	Other	Marketing Operations
None				

Format 8

Strength of Marketing Activities Needs

Need Type and Cause	How long has it existed?	How strong is it?	How valuable is it?	What is its impact?
None				

either product features or products. Your source for data will be your product analysis findings.

Marketing activities needs.

The final classification of needs is the manner in which you link your product offerings with a marketplace. In this situation you are dealing with needs that may occur as a result of either the organization of your marketing operations or the management of your marketing functions (sales, advertising, research, etc.). Format 7 addresses the origin of marketing activities needs, and Format 8 addresses their strength.

Your objective is to determine whether a need exists in your method of marketing products from the external market's point of view (usually customer based), from your internal product offerings point of view (product feature based or product type based), or from your internal management of all marketing-related activities. An example of need might come from a customer service, management, or telemarketing situation. Your source for data will be your marketing analysis findings.

Identifying Problems

A *problem* is defined as a force, usually negative in nature, in which something causes uncertainty or difficulty and is unwanted or requires an action for resolution. A problem can exist on it own or be created by some entity for someone else. An example of problem creation is the home compact disk (CD) industry. If the market had been left alone for consumers to decide when to begin using CD systems to listen to music, it would have taken years for the conversion to take place. But the music recording industry, record stores, and manufacturers of CD players got together and eliminated vinyl record albums, forcing consumers to purchase CDs and CD players. The result was the creation of a problem for consumers that was profitable for the CD industry.

Your goal is to identify the situation's problems and then establish how to resolve those problems. Then you must assess what that problem means to you in terms of value and how it might impact your marketing actions, positively or negatively. In identifying a situation's problems, you should divide your situation into the three situation areas: marketplace, product offerings, and marketing activities.

Remember that in addressing the issue of a problem, as a marketer you are interested not only in the problem itself and its origin, but also in how that problem translates into problems for your company to solve.

Marketplace problems.

When addressing problems that arise from the market itself, you are primarily looking, once again, at the customer element of the market structure. Usually a problem exists because customers are not being satisfied by either current products offered by the competition and your company, or alternatives. However, in the marketplace, problems can occur from many sources for many reasons. Suppliers, federal laws, and standard industry marketing methods are just a few of the elements that can create problems. Remember that although problems are usually negative, if resolvable, they can be profitable for your company.

Your objective is to assess whether a problem exists and whether you can resolve it. Your source for data will be your market analysis findings. Format 9 addresses the origin of market problems, and Format 10 addresses their strength. Remember that in assessing the market's problems, you are primarily concerned with patterns and trends of previous, present, and future customers.

Product offerings problems.

Another place where problems exist is in the products themselves, specifically your own products. In addressing the marketplace problems,

---

Format 9

Origin of Market Problems

	Basis of Problem			
Problem Type	Customer	Competition	Regulatory/Environmental	Other
Unfair selling conditions		*Yes—pricing wars*		

Format 10

Strength of Market Problems

Problem Type and Cause	How long has it existed?	How strong is it?	How valuable is it?	What is its impact?
Conditions— competitor's prices	*Last 3 years*	*Very strong—loss of sales*	*High—it cuts into profit margin*	*Loss of sales and revenues of 30%*

you are looking at existing conditions within the market structure. In addressing your products' problems, you are looking at your previous, present, and future offerings that may produce a problem. This type of problem comes from customers and their problems directly associated with your product offerings.

Your objective is to determine what type of problems customers may have—with your products only. You will need to add, modify, or delete either product features or products. Your source for data will be your product analysis findings. Format 11 addresses the origin of product problems and Format 12 addresses their strength.

Format 11

Origin of Product Problems

	Basis of Problem		
Problem Type	Product Feature	Product Benefit	Other
Defect in product			*Engineering limitation*

Format 12

Strength of Product Problems

Problem Type and Cause	How long has it existed?	How strong is it?	How valuable is it?	What is its impact?
Defect— poor R & D	*Forever, but just discovered*	*Medium strength*	*Not a safety issue, but return rates are high*	*Profitability from product re-issuing and poor image*

Marketing activities problems.

The final classification of problems is the manner in which you link your product offerings with the marketplace. In this situation, you are dealing with problems that may occur as a result of either the organization of your

---

Format 13

Origin of Marketing Activities Problems

	Basis of Problem			
Problem Type	External	Internal	Other	Marketing Operations
High sales turnover rate		*Yes—sales management function*		

Format 14

Strength of Marketing Activities Problems

Problem Type and Cause	How long has it existed?	How strong is it?	How valuable is it?	What is its Impact?
Turnover rate— low morale	*Last 2 years*	*Lost 23 salespeople in 2 years*	*Low sales and poor performance by sales staff*	*Other than inconsistent sales volume, image suffers as well*

---

marketing operations or the management of your marketing functions (sales, advertising, research, etc.).

Your objective is to determine whether a problem exists in your method of marketing products from the external market's point of view (usually customer based), from your internal product offerings point of view (product feature based or product type based), or from your internal management of all marketing-related activities. Your source for data will be your marketing analysis findings. Format 13 addresses the origin of marketing activities problems, and Format 14 addresses their strength.

Identifying Opportunities

An *opportunity* is defined as a force that can be both positive and negative in nature, in which something becomes favorable or advantageous due to a combination of uncontrollable and controllable circumstances. An opportunity can exist on its own or be created by some entity for someone else. Your goal is to identify the situation's opportunities and then establish how to take advantage of those opportunities. Then you must assess what that opportunity means to you in terms of value, and how it might impact your marketing actions positively or negatively. In identifying a situation's opportunities, you need to divide your situation into the three situation areas: marketplace, product offerings, and marketing activities.

Here is some marketing insight into the issue of opportunities: the trick is to first be aware of pending situations that might bear fruit. You should then try to influence any force that may prevent that opportunity from developing or assist it. You may be able to influence those forces in a way to position yourself to reap the benefits of those opportunities. Remember that in addressing the issue of opportunities, as a marketer you are interested not only in the opportunity itself and its origin, but also in how that opportunity translates into opportunities for your company to exploit.

An example of an opportunity is how some businesses experience government deregulating business. The government loosens up regulations to permit current players to avoid red tape and allows smaller, less powerful players to participate on a more equitable level. A marketer could influence that type of decision and then position itself to move quickly when the change takes effect; this could obtain great rewards for the company. The 1992 European market unification and the fall of communism in Eastern Europe demonstrate this idea.

Marketplace opportunities.
When addressing opportunities that arise from the market itself, you are looking at all elements of the market structure, not just customer elements as outlined in other components of this section. Opportunities can currently exist or they can be pending in nature. Many good opportunities are situations where forces are in place to create an opportunity and you, as a marketer, must discover them. Marketplace opportunities often arise not from luck, but from recognizing the various forces (man-made and natural) that change the way the marketplace is governed. A good marketer will view each market and determine its opportunities just by understanding what is possible based on resources of both the company and the market itself.

Your objective is to assess whether an opportunity exists or is pending and how you can take advantage of it. Your source for data will be your market analysis findings. Format 15 addresses the origin of market opportunities, and Format 16 addresses their strength. Remember that in assessing the market's opportunities, you are primarily concerned with patterns and trends of previous, present, and future customers.

Product offerings opportunities.
Another place where opportunities exist is in the products themselves, specifically your own products. In addressing the marketplace opportuni-

---

Format 15

Origin of Market Opportunities

| | Basis of Opportunities | | | |
Opportunity Type	Customer	Competition	Regulatory/Environmental	Other
New free-trade law			*Yes—FTC*	

Format 16

Strength of Market Opportunities

Opportunity Type and Cause	How long has it existed?	How strong is it?	How valuable is it?	What is its impact?
New law— open regulations	*Effective 1 year*	*Very strong—it gives us more new customers.*	*Growth rates will be high due to increased sales.*	*Although culture barriers exist, it will be worth the cost.*

---

ties, you are looking at existing conditions within the market structure. In addressing product opportunities, you are looking at your previous, present, and future offerings that may produce an opportunity. This type of opportunity comes from customers and their circumstances surrounding your product offerings. Format 17 addresses the origin of product opportunities, and Format 18 addresses their strength.

Your objective is to determine what type of opportunities exist or may exist—within your products only. You will need to add, modify, or delete either some product features or some products. Your source for data will be your product analysis findings.

Marketing activities opportunities.
The final classification of opportunities is the manner in which you link your product offerings with the marketplace. In this situation, you are

---

Format 17

Origin of Product Opportunities

	Basis of Opportunity		
Opportunity Type	**Product Feature**	**Product Benefit**	**Other**
New application for same product	*Yes—better alternative*	*Yes—cheaper solution*	

Format 18

Strength of Product Opportunities

Opportunity Type and Cause	How long has it existed?	How strong is it?	How valuable is it?	What is its Impact?
New use—new discovery	*Brand new*	*Very—only product on market*	*Pure product— 100% market share*	*Add sales and revenues of 300% over 1 year*

---

dealing with opportunities that may occur as a result of either the organization of your marketing operations or the management of your marketing functions (sales, advertising, research, etc.). Format 19 addresses the origin of marketing activities opportunities, and Format 20 addresses their strength.

Your objective is to determine whether an opportunity exists or may exist in your method of marketing products from the external market's point of view (usually customer based), from your internal product offerings point of view (product feature based or product type based), or from your internal management of all marketing-related activities. Your source for data will be your marketing analysis findings.

Format 19

Origin of Marketing Activities Opportunities

Opportunity Type	Basis of Opportunity			
	External	Internal	Other	Marketing Operations
Database creation		Yes—sales to advertising		Yes—research applications

---

Format 20

Strength of Marketing Activities Opportunities

Opportunity Type and Cause	How long has it existed?	How strong is it?	How valuable is it?	What is its impact?
Database—old customers, new applications	Completed in 6 months	Medium; enhance prospecting	Very efficient; low cost, fast sales	Generate additional revenue of $100,00 in first year of operation

---

INTERFACING ASSESSMENT FOR PLANNING

After completing the process of determining and assessing your current marketing situation, you are ready to interface that data with a strategic response. To this point, you have addressed your situation by viewing the elements of needs, problems, and opportunities. You classified those elements by three areas: marketplace, product offerings, and marketing activities. Now your objective is to draw conclusions regarding each one of those elements by reversing the three elements by those same three areas.

The purpose of this section is to first check your assessment findings against your conclusions to make sure they match. The other purpose of this section is to finally establish what is really happening in and outside of your marketing world. The final component is to transform that data into action by taking the situation elements and areas and outputting that data into the three marketing levels: strategic, departmental, and functional.

This activity bridges data collection, analysis, and assessment with planning. It prepares you for the actual strategic marketing planning process and aligns your assessment data with planning actions.

Throughout the entire section, you should keep in mind not only the identification of the situation elements, but also the qualification and prioritization of the elements. In other words, once you have established those elements, then you need to determine which ones are real and which ones are more important. Exhibit 2-2 displays how the entire process works: entering data from one format, converting that data via the situation assessment to another format, and translating that data into actions.

Exhibit 2-2
Format Interfaces

SITUATION	Needs	Problems	Opportunities	ACTION
Marketplace	Format 3, 4	Format 9, 10	Format 15, 16	Strategic Level
Product Offerings	Format 5, 6	Format 11, 12	Format 17, 18	Departmental Level
Marketing Activities	Format 7, 8	Format 13, 14	Format 19, 20	Functional Level

Assessment Conclusions

First, you should conclude what you believe your assessment findings represent. You do this by taking the 18 formats that you filled out with your overall assessment findings. Your objective is to pour those formats back into the three situation elements to verify your thoughts and to fully establish where you are today.

Marketplace assessment.
Format 21 summarizes the needs, problems, and opportunities that may exist in this situation area. Your objective is to review what you have learned regarding the origins and strengths of each situation element, alone and collectively. The result should be a determination (at a glance) and an assessment of where you stand in the marketplace.

150,376

Format 21

Marketplace Assessment

Importance (#)	Origins

Need:

#1 Customers' willingness to pay money for over-the-counter products, when alternatives exist.

Problem:

#3 Unfair competitive conditions exist due to competitor's undercutting of price, regardless of profit.

Opportunity:

#2 New free-trade law enacted by the Federal Trade Commission to stimulate GNP by selling goods to Japan.

	Strengths

Need:

#1 Customers' willingness to pay money has been historically very strong and causes a customer to purchase the product only after an extended decision process.

Problem:

#3 Competitor's pricing tactics over the last 3 years have caused us to lose 30% in sales, not to mention that our net margins are now only 1.2%.

Opportunity:

#2 Federal regulations have given us the right to sell our products abroad. This will provide us high growth rates, with some new costs in packaging due to cultural barriers.

Product offerings assessment.
Format 22 summarizes the needs, problems, and opportunities that may
exist in this situation area. Your objective is to review what you have
learned regarding the origins and strengths of each situation element, alone
and collectively. The result should be a determination (at a glance) and an
assessment of where you stand with the products you offer.

Format 22

Product Offerings Assessment

Importance (#)	Origins

Need:

#3 ABC product's ability to meet the needs of customers with current features.

Problem:

#1 Defect in product. The source was poor engineering and, as a result, the benefit to the user of this product has been reduced.

Opportunity:

#2 XYZ product has been discovered to have new applications. This new market offers an alternative that is better and cheaper.

Strengths

Need:

#3 Over the last 5 years, customer habits/preferences have shifted, causing them to look elsewhere. We have lost 30% in sales in that time, and because this product is a cornerstone, we need to either change or replace it.

Problem:

#1 Because of poor R&D testing, the product is perceived to have weak quality. Our image and our revenue stream have been hurt.

Opportunity:

#2 This "gold mine" will produce sales of $300,00 in 1 year (300% growth) and will provide a market share of 100% with only re-packaging as a cost to consider.

Marketing activities assessment.

Format 23 summarizes the needs, problems, and opportunities that may exist in this situation area. Your objective is to review what you have learned regarding the origins and strengths of each situation element, alone and collectively. The result should be a determination (at a glance) and an assessment of where you stand in the management of your marketing activities.

Format 23

Marketing Activities Assessment

Importance (#)	Origins

Need:

#3 None

Problem:

#1 Sales management had an unusually high turnover rate with the outside sales force.

Opportunity:

#2 A new database has been created. This new marketing tool will aid us in sales, advertising, and research.

	Strengths

Need:

#3 None

Problem:

#1 The turnover rate of the sales force has reached 23 over the past 2 years. Low morale among salespeople is due to poor support by the company (according to them). The result is poor sales and low customer opinion.

Opportunity:

#2 Database marketing has the potential to deliver new customers from current customer base, increasing our sales by 10% annually.

Final conclusions assessment.

Once you have determined and assessed each situation element, alone and collectively, you must come to a point where you commit to one of those identified situation elements in Format 24. In making your final conclusion, there are four exercises you need to perform before acting:

- Refinement of summary

- Product/market summary

Format 24

Final Conclusions Assessment

		Origins	
Importance	**#1**	**#2**	**#3**
Need:			
Situation Area:	*Marketplace (MP)*	*Product Offerings (PO)*	*Marketing Activities (MA)*
	Customers willing to pay money.	*ABC's ability to meet customers' needs.*	*None*
Problem:			
Situation Area:	*Product Offerings*	*Marketing Activities*	*Marketplace*
	Defect in product due to poor R&D	*High turnover rate in sales force*	*Unfair competition due to pricing*
Opportunity:			
Situation Area:	*Product Offerings*	*Marketplace*	*Marketing Activities*
	XYZ's new market application	*New trade bill with Japan*	*Database marketing capability*

- Marketing activities summary

- Final summary

Refinement of summary. The first part of forming a final conclusion of your situation assessment is even further refining. The purpose is to compare and isolate your needs, problems, and opportunities by the marketplace, product offerings, and marketing activities. Your objective is to review what you have learned regarding the origins and strengths and weaknesses, alone and collectively. The result should be a determination (at a glance) and an assessment of where you stand in your overall marketing endeavors.

In Format 25, you will match the origin with how strong or weak the origin is. It is a system of measuring the strength and weakness of each origin. The measurement uses a scale from 1 to 10, with 10 representing the highest degree. The basis for your measurement system is up to you; it can be a ranking (comparing one origin with another) or a rating (comparing an origin with a criterion you set independently). Regardless, your objective is to establish the degree of importance of each situation element. For example: Very Strong Strength, 10; Very Strong Weakness, 10 (i.e. not 1 equaling weak and 10 equaling strong).

Format 25

Ranking or Rating Origin Strengths or Weaknesses

System Used: *Ranking*

	Strengths/Weaknesses										
	1	2	3	4	5	6	7	8	9	10	
Need:											
1 *MP*	1	2	3	4	5	6	(7)	8	9	10	*Strong*
2 *PO*	1	2	3	4	5	(6)	7	8	9	10	*Strong*
3 *MA*	(1)	2	3	4	5	6	7	8	9	10	*Weak*
Problem:											
1 *PO*	1	2	3	4	(5)	6	7	8	9	10	*Weak*
2 *MA*	1	2	3	4	5	6	7	(8)	9	10	*Weak*
3 *MP*	1	2	3	4	5	6	(7)	8	9	10	*Weak*
Opportunity:											
1 *PO*	1	2	3	4	5	6	7	(8)	9	10	*Strong*
2 *MP*	1	2	3	4	5	6	7	8	(9)	10	*Strong*
3 *MA*	1	2	3	4	5	(6)	7	8	9	10	*Strong*

Product/market summary. The next step is to translate your assessment into a product-to-market linkage. Your objective is to convert what you have learned into principal situation areas to determine what initial courses your findings suggest.

    Exhibit 2-3 describes the options you may decide to exercise as a result of your findings. The objective is to search through your assessment findings and determine how you will apply those findings to model options.

Exhibit 2-3
Product/Market Direction
Model

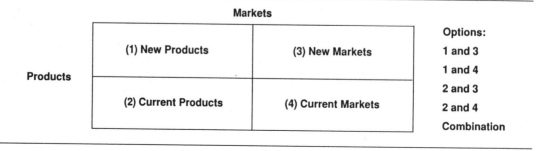

Marketing activities summary. As for the product/market summary, in the marketing activities summary you are trying to establish a linkage between this situation assessment and marketing actions. The product/market direction model is a method of establishing possible marketing opportunities, derived from the assessment. At best, the model demonstrates a possible avenue for increasing your profits.

Format 26 is designed to help you discover whether you can save money or need to spend more money in your marketing efforts. The objective is to search through your assessment findings and determine how you might apply those findings to the format. For each of your marketing activities (derived from your marketing analysis), take your overall operational duties and determine the change in percentage of sales you might make to those areas based on your assessment findings. The percentage represents marketing expenses as a percentage of sales volume. Your goal is to place a percentage value based on the estimated change you believe you could make. There is not a great range of change of percentage. Your total should be as close to zero as possible; a higher or lower number would indicate that you might be able to change the manner in which you market your products.

The format below is set up to first address "balance" in your marketing approach. That is why each marketing function has an equal number of combinations. The three columns represent three ways to view the degree of change (if any) your assessment findings may indicate. The three columns represent changing your marketing approach by decreasing (–), maintaining (0), or increasing (+). Within each column and marketing function, a range of numbers appears. These numbers measure the amount of change you will select, using the percentage of sales method. Your objective is to determine how you might spend your marketing dollars as a result of your findings. Will you simply reallocate your dollars, keeping your total budget the same? Will you increase your total budget to adjust each marketing function? These are just two questions out of several you need to consider.

Your side totals will be plus, minus, or zero, based on your assessment. Total the pluses and minuses and then combine the two; the difference is your possible change, if any.

Actually formulating a marketing budget (performed in your marketing plan) that matches the model is not your objective. Instead, this model is more a possible approach you might want to use, based on your analysis findings.

Final summary. The last part of this exercise is finalizing the entire process of your needs, problems, and opportunities assessment. It is here where you put to rest where you are and why things are happening to you. In addition, you need to establish what this section means to you in terms of what actions you will have to take to address your findings. Finally, you will decide whether these actions are worth the risk, money, and effort.

Format 26

Marketing Direction

Action:	Change (-) Decrease	No Change (0) Maintain	Change (+) Increase	Results (Sample) Total
Marketing Research	(10-1)	0	1-10	−3
Product Management	10-1	0	(1-10)	+2
Pricing	(10-1)	0	1-10	−1
Distribution	10-1	0	1-10	0
Sales Management	10-1	0	(1-10)	+1
Advertising	(10-1)	0	1-10	−1
Promotions	10-1	0	(1-10)	+2
Public Relations	(10-1)	0	1-10	−1
Legal Activities	10-1	0	(1-10)	+3
Operational Duties	(10-1)	0	1-10	−1

TOTAL		+8 −7 ———— +1%	+1%

Acting on Your Assessment

You have now completed your conclusions, and now you must link your assessment findings to the three situation levels. These levels will be your structure throughout the strategic marketing plan process. The purpose of this exercise is to prepare you to move to the next phase: formulating your mission.

Strategic marketing management level.

The strategic marketing management level deals with marketing at the corporate level. To simplify this book, the business unit level is also grouped with the corporate level. Most businesses today have one centralized management level; however, for companies with separate corporate and business unit operations, the strategic level process should be repeated and kept separate.

The strategic level focuses on the overall direction of marketing. Its emphasis is on the financial impact of marketing as it relates to the entire business structure. If the entire company is going through a strategic plan, this plan will become part of that plan. The strategic level will usually be handled by the executive vice president of marketing, or a similar position.

Departmental marketing management level.

The departmental marketing management level focuses on the actual department of marketing management. Its emphasis is on the operations of all marketing activities, and it establishes and monitors all marketing indicators (marketing costs, sales and revenues, market share, etc.) and strategies. This level is responsible for overseeing the activities of all nine functional areas (the marketing mix). The departmental level manages, implements, and controls all marketing actions and marketing personnel. It is usually handled by a marketing manager or director of marketing.

Functional marketing management level.

The functional marketing management level focuses on the actual, day-to-day operations of each of the nine marketing disciplines. As in the strategic level, many businesses will group various functions together, such as pricing with product management, or advertising with promotions and public relations. The functional managers work separately yet as a team to complement each function's assigned tasks. Each functional manager oversees budgeting, project scheduling, and staff activities. Functional marketing management is handled by the following positions:

- Research manager

- Product and brand managers

- Pricing manager

- Distribution manager

- Sales manager

- Advertising manager
- Promotions manager
- Public Relations manager
- Legal marketing manager

After each level has been defined to meet your specific situation, you will begin plugging your assessment findings into this structure. Your objective is to convert the assessment findings (needs, problems, and opportunities by marketplace, product offerings, and marketing activities) into actions that will affect your strategic, departmental, and functional marketing management levels. Upon completing Format 27, you are ready to place your assessment findings into a detailed, direction-driven strategic marketing plan.

Format 27

Needs, Problems, and Opportunities Summary

	Levels		
Importance	**Marketplace**	**Product Offerings**	**Marketing Activities**
Strategic:			
#1	Customers' willingness to pay money	XYZ's new market application	Database marketing usage
#2	New trade bill with Japan		
Departmental:			
#1	Unfair pricing by competition	Product defect in R&D	
#2		ABC's ability to meet customers' needs	
Functional:			
#1			High turnover rate in sales force
#2			

RESOURCE ASSESSMENT AND ALLOCATION

The final portion of the needs, problems, and opportunities assessment is identifying the resources to be called upon to make the necessary changes to your strategic plans. Although this section is somewhat out of the flow of assessment to planning, this are must be addressed to ensure that you are able to act. All of the information and accurate analysis in the world is virtually worthless unless you are able to do something about it. This section provides you with a structure for defining your resources (limits and capabilities) and your ability to make the proper changes.

Identifying Current and Future Limits

Limits are usually considered to be negative. In marketing, however, knowing your limits can not only save you from grief, but it can also make you more powerful because you are focusing strength on a particular item. You must first establish what your limits are, today and in the future. A limit is usually not permanent, so when establishing what you can and cannot do, keep in mind why the limit is there and how long it might be there. The bottom line is to determine what your various limitations are. You must understand what it takes to be a real player.

Internal limits.
Internal limits are factors that you can usually control. These limits are often financial, human resources, or physical (e.g., manufacturing facilities). Other limits will be marketing oriented, such as distribution or sales and service limits. Regardless of the nature of your internal limits, your objective is to identify their impact in acting on your assessment findings.

External limits.
External limits usually cannot be controlled. These limits are often conditions in the marketplace that prevent or make it difficult to take the proper action required. External limits can be very complex and require expensive remedies. Regardless of the nature of your external limits, your objective is to identify their impact in acting on your assessment findings.

Identifying Current and Future Capabilities

The opposite of *limits* is *capabilities*, which are positive in nature. Just as in defining your limit, capabilities are driven by factors that can be one way today and different tommorow. In assessing your capabilities, you must understand what it takes to be a real player and face whether or not you have what it takes to be a real player.

Internal capabilities.
Internal capabilities are those factors that you can usually control. Capabilities can be financial, human resources, or physical (e.g., manufacturing facilities). Other capabilities are marketing oriented, such as distribution or sales and service capabilities. Regardless of the nature of your internal capabilities, your objective is to identify their impact in acting on your assessment findings.

External capabilities.
External capabilities usually cannot be controlled. These capabilities are often conditions in the marketplace that provide or promote your ability to access a marketing situation. Although very few things are easy, external capabilities can help you take the proper action required. Regardless of the nature of your external capabilities, your objective is to identify their impact in acting on your assessment findings.

Your Ability to Change Your Actions

Once you have established your limits and your capabilities, you need to assess your ability to make and influence change. In strategic planning, your objective is not only to isolate elements that may be affecting your performance, but also to identify the correct treatment. This treatment usually comes from making decisions that will change a situation into a better situation.

Trying to change the way you do business is difficult. Businesses usually have a mindset that was established when the company was founded and when it peaked in performance. Change itself is as important, if not more important, than why the change is occurring. Your objective is to establish what you will need to change to meet the internal and external structure requirements.

Internal changes.

Defining your ability to affect the marketplace is a very important factor in strategic planning of any kind. Your objective is to determine how much you can change and whether that is enough to meet your situation findings. Then you must determine whether the amount of energy needed to respond is worth the returns.

External changes.

Defining the ability of the marketplace to change is a very important factor in strategic planning of any kind. Your objective in Format 28 is to determine how much the market will and can change and whether this is enough to meet your situation findings. Then you must predict when the changes will occur.

Format 28

Ability to Change Actions

	Limits	Capabilities	Changes
Internal	*Financial resources*	*Human resources*	*New financial sources*
External	*Geographic area served*	*None*	*Grow by expanding area*
Changes	*Expand*	*Maintain*	*Develop*

Unit 3

Formulating Your Mission Statement

You have now completed the initial activities in strategic planning—data collection, analysis, and assessing—and you are finally ready to begin developing your strategic marketing plan. In Unit 2, you identified situation elements in your marketplace, product offerings, and marketing activities. Now your goal is to translate these findings into actions. These actions are the contents of a strategic marketing plan:

- Mission statement

- Goals and objectives

- Strategies

- Control methods

WRITING YOUR MISSION STATEMENT

The first component of deciding on strategic actions is to establish your mission. Your mission is a translation of your current situation and perceived future, with the knowledge of your past, into a new course of action. You do this by writing a statement of a single sentence or no more than two paragraphs long. It doesn't matter if your company is small, with one product, or a large conglomerate with hundreds of products; your mission statement should be short, clear, and to the point.

Defining Your Mission

A mission establishes your identity, purpose, and the direction in which you are headed. A mission statement places a value on *who you are and what you do*. Once you have established this value, you can then create a statement that truly reflects what you have learned to this point about your situation and what you will do to increase your effectiveness as a result.

Purpose of the mission statement.
The purpose of the mission statement is to establish what your marketing efforts will be all about. These efforts must relate to your overall strategic

plan's mission statement. The mission statement gives you an identity by defining what will be your overall purpose for existing.

Value of the mission statement.
The value of a mission statement is that it explains to the reader in a qualitative and quantitative manner what you are worth. Everything you do from here—development of goals, objectives, strategies, and control— must be linked to this statement and reflect the statement's ideals.

Elements of the Mission Statement

A mission statement contains several elements. The first describes what you are all about and what direction you are headed. The other establishes your level of commitment for fulfilling your mission statement. This element defines the amount of effort and resources it will take to make your mission a success.

Description of your company.
In describing your firm, you should answer four questions:

- Who are you?

- What do you offer?

- Whom do you serve?

- Where will you serve?

These questions are simple, but it can be quite difficult to apply your situation assessment findings to a single, focused statement. This task becomes more complicated as you perform this exercise at three separate situation levels. Although your corporate (strategic level) statement will usually speak as your overall mission statement, each situation level should have its own separate mission. However, each level's mission statement should relate directly to the others.

Level of commitment.
In committing your efforts and resources, you establish what you are willing to put behind the mission statement to make it become a reality. Your objective is to decide how much of your financial, human, and physical resources you can afford to use. This information does not go into your formal plan in terms of the contents of the plan. However, you do want to keep track of this section throughout the process for later calculations.

MISSION STATEMENTS FOR EACH SITUATION LEVEL

To this point, you have learned what constitutes a mission statement. Now you are ready to apply that knowledge into the three marketing management levels for the strategic marketing plan. As stated earlier, each level will have its own mission, just as it will have its own goals, objectives, and strategies later on. You can consider, however, that the strategic level represents your overall mission as well as that particular level. Exhibit 3-1 on the following page shows how the mission statements for the three levels work together.

Strategic Marketing Management Level

Your mission theme at the strategic marketing management level should reflect your marketing actions at the corporate and/or business unit levels. This means that your description and your level of commitment should be geared to that level. It has already been stated that this level should reflect not only strategic thoughts, but also your overall marketing thoughts. Items such as growth, financial return, budget control, and product/market opportunities should be covered. After completing Format 29, you should construct a narrative mission statement using this information.

Format 29

Strategic Marketing Management Mission Statement

Variable	Interpretation
Who are you?	*We are a consumer package products company.*
What do you offer?	*We offer products targeted at homemakers who care about cleaning their homes.*
Whom do you serve?	*We serve homemakers who are educated, married with children, with household incomes above $30,000.*
Where will you serve?	*We serve homemakers who live and shop in the U.S. and Canada.*

Level of commitment

Your strategic marketing management commitment level should focus on the financial obligations that it will take to make this level work. In Format 30, you will establish what you are willing to invest to make this plan a success.

Format 30

Strategic Marketing Management Commitment Level

Variable	Interpretation
Financial Resources	*20% increase of $10,000 over the next two years.*
Human Resources	*Retain current work force with two new V.P.s.*
Physical Resources	*Expand facility to 3,000 sq. ft. of office space.*

Exhibit 3-1
Sample Mission Statements

Levels:	Mission:
Strategic	Establish a proactive organization that markets auto accessories to U.S. do-it-yourself customers in the U.S.
Departmental	Establish a proactive marketing approach that provides solid sales and revenue from auto accessories.
Functional	Establish proactive sales and promotions actions for auto accessories.

Departmental Marketing Management Levels

Your mission theme at the departmental marketing management level should reflect your marketing actions at the department level. This means that your description and your level of commitment should be geared to that level. You should describe your actual marketing management operations. Items such as sales, profitability, target marketing, and market share should be covered. After completing Format 31, you should construct a narrative mission statement using this information.

Format 31

Departmental Marketing Management Mission Statement

Variable	Interpretation
Who are you?	*We provide products that are safe and profitable for the company.*
What do you offer?	*We produce home cleaning products that are researched and tested.*
Whom do you serve?	*We serve our current and future customers who desire multipurpose products that solve their needs.*
Where will you serve?	*We serve customers who live and work in the U.S. and Canada.*

Level of commitment

Your departmental marketing management commitment level should focus on the financial obligations that it will take to make this level work. In Format 32, you will establish what you are willing to invest to make this plan a success.

Format 32

Departmental Marketing Management Commitment Level

Variable	Interpretation
Financial Resources	
Human Resources	
Physical Resources	

Functional Marketing Management Levels

Your mission theme at the functional marketing management level should reflect your marketing actions at the marketing function level. This means that your description and your level of commitment should be geared to that level. Items such as individual projects of each functional group, key daily tasks, expenses, and scheduling/implementation actions should be covered. After completing Format 33, you should construct a narrative mission statement using this information.

Format 33

Functional Marketing Management Mission Statement

Variable	Interpretation
Who are you?	*We are one of the external communication arms of the marketing department.*
What do you offer?	*We supply the marketing department with the message and medium to get customers to act (purchase).*
Whom do you serve?	*We serve customers who learn of products through mass marketing media usage.*
Where will you serve?	*We serve customers who live in the U.S. and Canada.*

Level of commitment.

Your functional marketing management commitment level should focus on the financial obligations that it will take to make this level work. In Format 34, you will establish what you are willing to invest to make this plan a success.

Format 34

Functional Marketing Management Commitment Level

Variable	Interpretation
Financial Resources	
Human Resources	
Physical Resources	

Unit 4

Formulating Your Goals and Objectives

Once you have defined who you are, you then need to define where you want to go. You do this by establishing goals and objectives corresponding to your situation assessment findings and your mission statement. Goals and objectives take your findings and establish what you want to address about those findings. Although goals and objectives are often thought of as the same, they are two separate actions. However, in setting one, you need to set the other; therefore, they are defined together in this exercise.

DEFINING YOUR GOALS

A *goal* is a general statement of desired direction or improvement. Goals determine points to achieve, whereas objectives are more specific and bring detailed measurement to each goal. The most effective goal setting is done by establishing two general time frames: short-term and long-term. These goal levels are performed concurrently.

Identifying Your Goals

The first thing you do in determining your goals is to establish where you are headed and what you expect to gain when you get there. Then you must establish your timetable for making this journey. You do this by selecting a new course of action. In forming this course, you again look at your situation assessment findings (needs, problems, and opportunities) and your mission statement. You are basically converting these findings into actions. Format 35 provides a space for you to establish your goals.

In identifying your goals, the first thing you must make clear is what point (designation) you desire to reach and why. The "why" has, of course, already been answered because it is a need, problem, or opportunity element you have selected. The point is the act in which you obtain those elements. What you will want is key; however, knowing why you want it (to respond to a situation element) is just as key. To want something means there must be a reason. In constructing your goals, your description (which is general in nature), is based on what you *want to obtain and when you want to obtain it.*

Format 35

Establishing Your Strategic Marketing Management Goals

Variable	Interpretation	Expected Gains
What do you want to obtain?	*More profits through marketing*	*Increased income for reinvestment into product development*
When do you want to obtain it?	*Within next 2 years*	

Interpretation	Short-Term Time Frame	Long-Term Time Frame
	Yes—2 years	*Yes—beyond*

**Exhibit 4-1
Strategic Marketing
Planning Process**

Exhibit 4-1 shows how the analysis findings are linked to goals/objectives and strategy building.

	Analysis	Mission	Goals/Objectives	Strategy
Example:	*Poor gross profit margins*		*Solid gross profit margin of 38%*	*Establish new pricing policies.*

A part of identifying goals is how the goal will resolve, meet, or take advantage of your situation assessment findings. In other words, what will the goal accomplish? The purpose of setting a goal is not only to obtain a desired element, but also to improve your current situation. Each improvement must be tied-on to whatever goal you establish.

**Your Time Frame for
Achieving Goals**

Depending on the amount of detail you would like to devote to your goals, placing your goals in long-term and short-term formats can be beneficial. Whether you are trying to obtain these goals concurrently or you are prioritizing the goals, this format is a good way to approach goal setting. Depending on the number of goals you identify, each goal should be linked to a time frame, and each time frame should be attached to an achievement.

Short-term goals.
Short-term goals focus on areas that need immediate attention or are emergencies. These goals should work together and be realistic—obtainable with currently available resources or resources that could be obtained from accessible outside resources. Short-term goals are usually set to be achieved within one or two years.

Long-term goals.
Long-term goals usually are focused on areas that represent growth or expansion. These goals should work together and be realistic—obtainable with currently available resources or resources that could be obtained from accessible outside resources. Long-term goals are set to be achieved in three to five years.

DEFINING YOUR OBJECTIVES

After you have defined where you want to be and when you want to get there, you need to add more detail. You do this by establishing objectives that represent your goals, and by determining measurement and types of accomplishments. As with goal setting, you must then attach a time frame to each objective.

Identifying Your Objectives

An *objective* is a specific, measurable statement that supports your goals with further detail by translating these goals into marketing achievements. Objectives should reflect your goal's purpose by establishing reachable outcomes. In establishing your objectives, you should determine how the outcome will be measured and note various achievement milestones.

Outcome measurement.
Measurement is based on two variables: activity and rate of increase (improvement).

Achievement milestones.
Once you have determined your expected outcome and the manner in which it will be measured, then you need to set milestones for each variable. Although it can be said that these milestones are linked to time frames (short-term and long-term), milestones are separate. They are measuring points within time periods, not defined by dates. Each milestone represents an achievement or accomplishment set by the design of your objectives. Milestones provide accountability so objectives can be evaluated for accuracy. This will help you later in measuring results and establishing appraisal criteria. Measurement is based on two variables: indicator and rate of increase (improvement).

Your Time Frame for Achieving Objectives

Objectives should be matched with long-term and short-term time frames, and they should also reflect your goal's time frame. These objectives should be performed concurrently and should be specific.

Short-term objectives.
Short-term objectives focus on areas that need immediate attention or are emergencies. Objectives should work together and be realistic—obtainable with currently available resources, or resources that could be obtained from accessible outside resources. Short-term objectives are usually set to be achieved within one or two years.

Long-term objectives.

Long-term objectives are usually focused on areas that represent growth or expansion. These objectives should work together and be realistic—obtainable with currently available resources, or resources that could be obtained from accessible outside resources. Long-term objectives are usually set to be achieved within three to five years.

OBJECTIVES VERSUS FORECASTS

As you approach each situation level, goals and objectives will need to be established. Part of setting objectives can be establishing marketing forecasts and projections. However, objectives are founded on "desired achievement" (a realistic wish for obtainment), whereas forecasts are more founded on "predictive achievement" (realistic expectations or estimates for obtainment). Whether you include forecasts and projections in your strategic marketing plan is up to you.

Many marketers believe that setting objectives for one to five years is acceptable, but placing a dollar figure or confirming actual activities is not acceptable in such a long time frame. Other marketers believe that forecasting is the role of the annual marketing plan. This is acceptable, but a marketing plan is designed to be completed and used one year at a time. Thus the issue of desiring marketing forecasts for more than one year must be resolved.

Regardless of where you decide to include forecasts, it is advisable to include them at the strategic and departmental marketing management levels. Formats for those forecasts are included in *Preparing the Marketing Plan* in this series. You can either obtain them and modify them to reflect the time frames you desire (one year to five years) or design your own forecast models. If you choose the latter, you should track dollars and units (by product and overall product line) by year, and the percentage of growth from year to year. Your options, as a result, are to put your forecast with your objectives, create a separate document on a five-year format, or take your marketing plan and simply duplicate it for five years.

For the purpose of presenting your objectives, you will need to merge both activity and indicator variables to produce a statement form. The indicators are also used separately from your report to verify your original objectives and monitor their effectiveness.

GOALS AND OBJECTIVES FOR EACH SITUATION LEVEL

You have now learned what goals and objectives are; now you are ready to apply that knowledge in three marketing management levels for the strategic marketing plan. As stated earlier, each level will have its own goals and objectives, just as it has its own mission statement and its own strategies.

Strategic Marketing Management Level

Your goals and objectives at the strategic marketing management level should reflect your marketing actions at the corporate and/or business unit levels. This means that your goals and objectives should be geared to that level. This level should reflect not only strategic thoughts, but also your overall marketing thoughts. Your goals should be general in description but specific in origin. Your objectives should be specific in both description and origin. Listed below are examples of objectives that could be used:

- Sales volume

- Financial impact of product sold

- Cost of marketing controls (costs vs. income)

- Business expansion/growth (gross product output)

- Return on investment/product profitability

- Customer satisfaction

- Image (position as viewed by market)

You will establish your objectives by targeting specific activities, rate of increase (percentage), and a time frame (short-term or long-term). Many activities could be used to describe your objectives; listed below are examples of goals with corresponding objectives:

(Strategic level)
Goals: Example Possibilities

- *Increased sales volume.*

- *Cost control of marketing.*

(Strategic level)
Objectives: Examples (Statement from topics)

- *Maintain return on investment of 30% from product sales.*

- *Expand growth rate by 2% to 5% in annual revenues to offset increased rate of marketing costs.*

Format 36 will help you formulate goals and objectives together to produce well-thought-out points of achievement at the strategic level and understand how the remaining levels reflect them. That is not to say that each level does not have its own separate goals and objectives; but if the upper levels establish goals and objectives, the lower levels must also respond with goals and objectives that reflect this level. You will target specific indicators and note the desired rate of increase (percentage) and time frame (short-term or long-term). Many indicators could be used to describe your objectives; the following are several examples:

- Sales volume
- Revenue volume
- Cost of marketing expenses
- Product profitability performance
- Rate of return on investment

Format 36

Strategic Marketing Management Objectives

Outcome Measurement—Activity

Variable	By __8__ % Increase	Time Frame
Raise prices on all products (average).		*By the end of next year.*

Achievement Milestones—Indicators

Variable	By __10__ % Increase	Milestones
Obtain an average gross profit margin of 39% on all products.		*Over 1 year, with a 6-month milestone check.*

Summary

	Goal	Objective
Need:		
Problem: *Poor profits*	*Improve profit margins.*	*Obtain better profit margin through higher prices.*
Opportunity:		

Departmental Marketing Management Levels

Your goals and objectives at the departmental marketing management level should reflect your marketing actions at the department level. This means that your goals and objectives should be geared to that level. Your goals in Format 37 should be general in description but specific in origin. Your objectives in Format 38 should be specific in both description and origin. Listed below are examples of objectives that could be used:

- Sales forecasting
- Revenue forecasting
- Cost of marketing projections

Format 37

Establishing Your Departmental Marketing Management Goals

Variable	Interpretation	Expected Gains
What do you want to obtain?	*Increase revenues through higher prices*	*Larger profits*
When do you want to obtain it?	*Within the next 6 months.*	

Interpretation	Short-Term Time Frame	Long-Term Time Frame
Increase revenues	*6 months* *Yes*	——

Format 38

Departmental Marketing Management Objectives

Outcome Measurement—Activity

Variable	By __8__ % Increase	Time Frame
Generate additional revenues by units sold.		*Within the next year*

Achievement Milestones—Indicators

Variable	By __10__ % Increase	Milestones
Maintain price levels that produce an average gross profit margin of 39%.		*Over a 1-year period with quarterly milestone checks.*

Summary

	Goal	Objective
Need:		
Problem: *Poor profits*	*Better per-unit sales/revenues*	*Increase pricing levels on each unit sold.*
Opportunity:		

- Market share and penetration

- Market expansion (market size)

- Positioning perceptions

- Target market options/selections

- Overall operations and organization management

You will establish your objectives by targeting specific activities, rate of increase (percentage), and a time frame (short-term or long-term). Many activities could be used to describe your objectives; listed below are examples of goals with corresponding objectives:

(Strategic level)
Goals: Example Possibilities

- *Increased sales volume.*

- *Cost control of marketing.*

(Departmental level)
Objectives: Examples (Statement from topics)

- *Increase sales of products by 5% to a total of 8% annually.*

- *Establish strict guidelines for marketing department's budget.*

As noted earlier, if you wish to attach, for example, a sales forecast with your objectives, this is an acceptable place. However, you will need to adopt your own formats.

You will establish your objectives by targeting specific indicators, rate of increase (percentage), and a time frame (short-term or long-term). Many indicators could be used to describe your objectives; listed below are several examples:

- Product sales

- Product revenues

- Product profits

- Marketing expenses (activities and operations)

Functional Marketing Management Levels

Your goals and objectives at the functional marketing management level should reflect your marketing actions at the function level. This means that your goals and objectives should be geared to that level. Your goals in Format 39 should be general in description but specific in origin. Your objectives in Format 40 should be specific in both description and origin. The following are examples of objectives that could be used:

Format 39

Establishing Your Functional Marketing Management Goals

Variable	Interpretation	Expected Gains
What do you want to obtain?	*Re-established pricing structure*	*More income on per-unit sales*
When do you want to obtain it?		

Interpretation	Short-Term Time Frame	Long-Term Time Frame
Pricing structure	*Yes*	———

- Marketing research

- Product management and development

- Pricing and financial control

- Distribution

- Sales management (selling activity)

- Advertising

- Promotions

- Public relations

- Legal marketing activities

You will establish your objectives by targeting specific activities, rate of increase (percentage), and a time frame (short-term or long-term). Many activities could be used to describe your objectives; listed below are examples of goals with corresponding objectives:

(Strategic level)
Goals: Example Possibilities

- *Increased sales volume.*

- *Cost control of marketing.*

(Functional level)
Objectives: Examples (Statement from topics)

- *Increase sales quotas by 10%.*

- *Maintain each function's budgets within 2% of the most current budget.*

Format 40

Functional Marketing Management Objectives

Outcome Measurement—Activity

Variable	By __8__ % Increase	Time Frame
Adjust pricing on all products.		*Within 3 months*

Achievement Milestones—Indicators

Variable	By __10__ % Increase	Milestones
Retain a per-unit price that will produce an average gross profit of 39%.		*Over the next 6 months with monthly milestone checks*

Summary

	Goal	Objective
Need:		
Problem: *Poor profits*	*New pricing structure*	*More profits through higher prices*
Opportunity:		

You will establish your objectives by targeting specific indicators, rate of increase (percentage), and a time frame (short-term or long-term). Many indicators could be used to describe your objectives; listed below are several examples:

- Expense control (on budget)

- Scheduling (on time)

- Project performance (results appraisals)

- Productivity and efficiency

- Capability enhancements

INTERACTION AMONG MARKETING MANAGEMENT LEVELS

To demonstrate how each marketing management level works together in determining objectives using outcome measurement, you will use the examples provided in this section. Exhibit 4-2 displays how it all links together.

Exhibit 4-2

Strategic Level Goal: Increased Sales Volume

Objective/Outcome Measurement

Strategic Level: *Maintain return on investment of 30% from product sales.*

Departmental Level: *Increase sales of products by 5% to a total of 8% annually.*

Functional Level: *Increase sales quotas by 10%.*

Another way to view goals and objectives is that they are created to work together and still address their own level's requirements. The following example for Format 41 establishes how your goals and objectives at the three situation levels work together in preparation for corresponding strategies. This format will be used again at the end of the strategy formulation section for this same reason.

Format 41

Composite View Summary

| | Levels | | |
	Strategic	Departmental	Functional
Goal	*Expand business.*	*Expand sales base (offerings).*	*Expand sales area.*
Objective	*Increase growth of products by generating additional sales to reach a growth rate of 5% annually.*	*Increase product sales by 5% to 10% annually.*	*Increase sales quotas by 10% per year.*

Unit 5

Formulating Your Marketing Strategy

The next step in the strategic marketing planning process is formulating your strategy. Unit 5 deals with taking your situation findings, your corresponding mission statement, and your goals and objectives and turning these elements into actions.

DEFINING YOUR MARKETING STRATEGY

Now that you have stated your marketing intentions, you need to determine how you will achieve these goals and objectives, working within your mission. In identifying your marketing strategies, your goal is to select and establish actions that will allow you to achieve your goals and objectives using the most cost-effective and efficient method possible. Although the overall approach is process-based, marketing is still an inexact science. As a result, you must have sensitivity as well as hard numbers to decide on the proper actions.

Defining Your Market Strategy

A *strategy* is a thought process of command that responds to acquiring a particular point, and the plan of action resulting from that thought process. In defining what a strategy does, you must examine its purpose and describe how it works.

Purpose.
The purpose of strategy in the marketing environment is to establish the process you design and follow in your journey to obtain your designated goals and objectives. Although carrying out these strategies (implementation) is the responsibility of actual plans (e.g., a marketing plan), your goal is to determine the proper course.

Description.
Strategy formulation begins with taking your desired outcomes from your previous goals and objectives formulations and then establishing your ability to best obtain those outcomes and developing the method in which you

will obtain them. A strategy is simply the set of decisions that defines the overall marketing approach that will be followed to achieve the goals you have established. Strategies will then be refined into specific tactics and action plans, which are linked to specific timetables.

These specific tactics (the actual actions) will be established in the strategic marketing plan in overall terms, but the actual "hard-core" implementation of these tactics will be the responsibility of the annual marketing plan. In formulating your strategy, you will break it down into a series of tactical moves. You don't need to be concerned with implementing these tactics, however. Your annual marketing plans will cover who will complete each task and when.

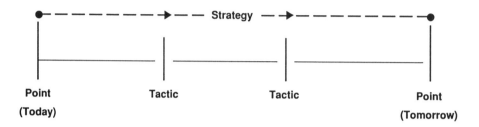

Elements of the Marketing Strategy

The three basic elements that comprise a marketing strategy are structure (action), time frame, and project/task implementation. Each marketing management level will vary in terms of the actual components of each element, but they will share an overall strategy.

Strategy structure.
This element establishes the variables that drive your strategic marketing plan. The variables listed below govern how a strategy will function:

- Budget allocation

- Activities for action (core variable)

- Project/task assigning

- Measurement of performance

You must have a strategy to govern each goal and objective. Although an overriding strategy is common, separate and specific strategies must assist an overall strategy. Budget allocation addresses the funding that will be committed to this effort, as well as determining how much it will cost to perform your strategies. Activities for action focus on the actual methods you will employ in obtaining your goals and objectives. Project/task assigning deals with determining who is in charge of what, and who reports to whom. Measurement of performance is simply monitoring the effectiveness of your actions. The soul of your planning must be accountability.

Time frame.

The time frame elements refer to the window of opportunity you must work under to accomplish your strategy activities. In your goals and objectives, you established these time frames; in developing your strategies, they must match. Again, time frames may be short-term or long-term.

Project/task implementation.

This element is different from the previous time frame element because it concentrates on the actual implementation of your actions within the time frames selected. Each strategy you develop will need to be linked to an action or tactic. Three variables that comprise this element are: timetable coordination, scheduling of actions, and benchmark control.

MARKETING STRATEGIES FOR EACH SITUATION LEVEL

Now that you have learned what constitutes a strategy, you are ready to apply that knowledge in the three marketing management levels for the strategic marketing plan. As stated earlier, each level has its own strategies, just as it has its own mission statement and goals and objectives.

Strategic Marketing Management Level Strategies

Your strategy theme for the strategic marketing management level should reflect your marketing actions at the corporate and/or business unit levels. This means that your strategies should be geared to that level. The strategic marketing management level strategies should reflect not only strategic thoughts, but also your overall marketing thoughts. Your strategies should be specific in origin.

Strategy structure.

This component states how you will respond to the goals and objectives set at this level. At the strategic level, you are concerned with the following strategies:

* Sales volume

* Revenue generation

* Marketing cost controls (costs vs. income)

* Business expansion/growth (gross product output)

* Return on investment

* Customer satisfaction

* Image (as viewed by market)

Once you have established what you need to respond to, you then begin to form your marketing strategies, such as the following:

- Goal:

  Expand business.

- Objectives:

  Generate additional sales to reach a growth rate of 5% annually.

- Strategy:

  Using external means, form a business relationship with a similar business in the international marketplace to produce and sell products and share in the financial rewards.

- Tactic:

  Develop a joint venture with ABC Company to market Brand X in Europe by April of next year.

As you are structuring your marketing strategies, ask yourself what source you will use to form your strategies and tactics. Often the goals and objectives themselves will provide you with data that you can simply reverse and expand upon. Other options come from experience and business sense. Commercial marketing case study books and strategy development books are available, but most of the time the source you will cite will be your marketing planning activities. You can access this information by either going back to *Evaluating Marketing Strengths and Weaknesses* or forward to *Preparing a Marketing Plan* in the *AMA Marketing Toolbox* series.

Structuring your strategy at the strategic level.
You are now able to begin formulating your strategy structure. To do this, you must be able to respond to your goals and objectives and deliver the recommended actions. You need to build a foundation for your strategies. This foundation is made up of the variables outlined in the definition of strategy structure. The formats in this unit will provide you with a method of considering the best way to approach building your structure.

Format 42 addresses budget allocation by displaying your funding commitment and cost to deliver your strategy. These two variables should match; if they don't, you need to rethink your strategies formulation process. Format 43 addresses activities for action. For every strategy, there must be one or more tactics. Format 44 addresses project/task assigning. Someone must be in charge of everything that is established and carried out. Format 45 addresses measurement of your performance. Every activity undertaken must be accountable by some measurable improvement. This should indicate how (by what method) you will check yourself. In other words, how effective will you be/were you at obtaining your goals/objectives and/or forecasts?

Format 42

Budget Allocation for Strategic Level (Five-Year Time Frame)

Goal/Objective: _____ *Expand business* _____

Variable	Strategy ($)	Tactic ($)	Tactic ($)
Funding Commitment (Cost to Deliver Strategy)	*10,000*	*5,000*	*8,000*

Format 43

Activities for Action for Strategic Level

Variable	Goal/Objective: _____ *Expand business* _____

Strategy *Using external means, form joint venture with a company that is similar in nature to sell a product.*

Tactic *Market internationally a "private labeled" product by April.*

Tactic

Format 44

Project/Task Assigning for Strategic Level

Goal/Objective: _____ *Expand business* _____

Variable	Strategy	Tactic	Tactic
Management/Control	*A. Smith*	*B. Johnson*	
Reporting	*A. Smith to C. Jones*	*B. Johnson to A. Smith*	

Format 46 is a method of verifying your thoughts regarding your strategy structuring approach. This format places activities for action against the other three strategy structure variables. It will help you establish strategies that truly are effective and will produce the desired results. (This format would not be used in the final document for presentation.)

Time Frame.

Part of establishing a strategy structure is determining which strategy will work in which time frame. Marketing management levels will differ in time sensitivity depending on what goals and objectives were set and what type of strategy has been formed. Format 49 displays how you can take your strategy structure and place it within a specific time period.

Format 45

Measurement of Performance for Strategic Level

Goal/Objective: _____ *Expand business* _____

Variable	Strategy	Tactic	Tactic
Results Appraisal			
Financial	X	X	
Organization			
Product Value/Performance	X	X	
Quality Control			
Public Opinion			
Marketing Capabilities			
Market Presence	X	X	
Other			

Format 46

Structure Verification for Strategic Level

Goal/Objective: _____ *Expand business* _____

Variable	Budget Allocation	Project/Task Assigning	Measurement of Performance
Point (A): *Low sales*	———	———	———
Strategy *Joint venture*	10,000	*A. Smith*	*Financial, product value, and market presence*
Tactic *New product line*	5,000	*B. Johnson*	*Financial, product value, and market presence*
Tactic *New market entered*	8,000	*B. Johnson*	*Financial, product value, and market presence*
Point (B): *Improved sales*	———	———	———

A: Where you are now

B: Where you want to go

Format 47

Time Frame for Strategic Level

Variable	Goal and Objectives:	*Expand business*

Short-Term Strategies

Strategy #1   *Push present product line.*

Strategy

Long-Term Strategies

Strategy #2 *Introduce new products via a joint venture alliance.*

Strategy

Project/task implementation.

The final component of this situation level's marketing strategy is determining how each strategy and tactic will be turned into action. The project/task implementation component puts the wheels in motion to convert strategy into actual activities. Although the actual tactics of a particular strategy will be established, actual implementation will be included in the marketing plan. However, you are concerned with the bridge between thought and action, and that is where this component comes in.

Format 48 will help you establish project/task timetable coordination that will allow you to place a date with an action.

Format 48

Project/Task Timetable Coordination for Strategic Level

19 _____

	Jan.	Feb.	March	April	May	June	July	Aug.	Sept.	Oct.	Nov.	Dec.
Strategy #1	*X* ———————————————————————————											
Strategy #2					*X* ———————————————————————							

In Format 49, benchmark control acts as a safety net to allow you to check how you are doing along the way and at the end. Its purpose is to give you a final device to make sure you are on track.

Format 49

Benchmark Control for Strategic Level

	Evaluation Point (Date/Time)	Action (Safeguard)	Re-initiate Option
Strategy	*1 year*	*Sales report*	*No*
Strategy	*1 year*	*Operations report*	*Yes*

Departmental Marketing Management Level Strategies

Your strategy theme for the departmental marketing management level should reflect your marketing actions at the department level. This means that your strategies should be geared to that level. Your strategies should be specific in origin.

Strategy structure.

This component states how you will respond to the goals and objectives set at this level. At the departmental level, you are concerned with the following strategies:

- Sales forecasting

- Revenue forecasting

- Cost of marketing projections

- Market share and penetration

- Market expansion (market size)

- Positioning perceptions

- Target market options/selections

- Overall operations and organization management

Once you have established what you need to respond to, you then begin to form your marketing strategies, such as the following:

- Goal:

Expand sales base (product offerings).

- Objectives:

  Increase product sales by 5% to 10% annually.

- Strategy:

  Develop criteria for selecting which company to approach for the joint venture.

- Tactic:

  Obtain signed contracts with ABC Company and set up marketing system to market our version of Brand X.

Structuring your strategy at the departmental level.
You are now able to begin formulating your strategy structure. To do this, you must be able to respond to your goals and objectives and deliver the recommended actions. You need to build a foundation for your strategies. This foundation is made up of the variables outlined in the definition of strategy structure. As needed, use Formats 50–65 from Unit 2 for this part.

Format 50 addresses budget allocation by displaying your funding commitment and cost to deliver your strategy. These two variables should match; if they don't, you need to rethink your strategies formulation process. Format 51 addresses activities for action. For every strategy, there must be one or more tactics. Format 52 addresses project/task assigning. Someone must be in charge of everything that is established and carried out. Format 53 addresses measurement of your performance. Every activity undertaken must be accountable.

Format 54 is a method of verifying your thoughts regarding your strategy structuring approach. This format places activities for action against the other three strategy structure variables. It will help you establish strategies that truly are effective and will produce the desired results.

Time frame.
Part of establishing a strategy structure is determining which strategy will work in which time frame. Marketing management levels will differ in time sensitivity depending on what goals and objectives were set and the type of strategy that has been formed. Format 55 displays how you can take your strategy structure and place it within a specific time period.

Project/task implementation.
The final component of this situation level's marketing strategy is determining how each strategy and tactic will be turned into action. The project/task implementation component puts the wheels in motion to convert strategy into actual activities. Although the actual tactics of a particular strategy will be established, actual implementation will be included in the marketing plan. However, you are concerned with the bridge between thought and action, and that is where this component comes in.

Format 56 will help you establish project/task scheduling that will allow you to place a date with an action.

In Format 57, benchmark control acts as a safety net to allow you to check how you are doing along the way and at the end. Its purpose is to give you a final device to make sure you are on track.

Functional Marketing Management Level Strategies

Your strategy theme for the functional marketing management level should reflect your marketing actions at the functional level. This means that your strategies should be geared to that level. Your strategies should be specific in origin.

Strategy structure.

This component states how you will respond to the goals and objectives set at this level. At the functional level, you are concerned with the following strategies:

- Marketing research

- Product management and development

- Pricing and financial control

- Distribution

- Sales management (selling)

- Advertising

- Promotions

- Public relations

- Legal marketing activities

Within each one of these activities are where your strategies really lie. Even subcomponents of each activity can supply you with tactics. Please note that unlike the strategic and departmental levels, the functional level is broken down into nine functions. As a result, you will need to take the formats provided and apply them to each functional area that is applicable to your situation.

Once you have established what you need to respond to, you then begin to form your marketing strategies, such as the following:

- Goal:

  Expand sales area.

- Objectives:

  Increase sales quotas by 10% a year.

- Strategy:

  Introduce a new addition to the product line by acquiring a new product using outside means.

- Tactic:

  Enhance the attractiveness of new products versus Brand X by lowering the price of our version.

Structuring your strategy at the functional level.
You are now able to begin formulating your strategy structure. To do this, you must be able to respond to your goals and objectives and deliver the recommended actions. You need to build a foundation for your strategies. This foundation is made up of the variables outlined in the definition of strategy structure.

Format 58 addresses budget allocation by displaying your funding commitment and cost to deliver your strategy. These two variables should match; if they don't, you need to rethink your strategies formulation process. Format 59 addresses activities for action. For every strategy, there must be one or more tactics. Format 60 addresses project/task assigning. Someone must be in charge of everything that is established and carried out. Format 61 addresses measurement of your performance. Every activity undertaken must be accountable.

Format 62 is a method of verifying your thoughts regarding your strategy structuring approach. This format will help establish strategies that truly are effective. It places activities for action against the other three strategy structure variables.

Time frame.
Part of establishing a strategy structure is determining which strategy will work in which time frame. Marketing management levels will differ in time sensitivity depending on what goals and objectives were set and the type of strategy that has been formed. Format 63 displays how you can take your strategy structure and place it within a specific time period.

Project/task implementation.
The final component of this situation level's marketing strategy is determining how each strategy and tactic will be turned into action. The project/task implementation component puts the wheels in motion to convert strategy into actual activities. Although the actual tactics of a particular strategy will be established, actual implementation will be included in the marketing plan. However, you are concerned with the bridge between thought and action, and that is where this component comes in.

Format 64 will help you establish project/task scheduling that will allow you to place a date with an action.

In Format 65, benchmark control acts as a safety net to allow you to check how you are doing along the way and at the end. Its purpose is to give you a final device to make sure you are on track.

FINAL COMPOSITE VIEW

Format 66 will help you truly understand the entire system of strategy formulation. Unlike Format 41 in Unit 4, where you listed only a goal at the strategic level and the corresponding objectives defined by each marketing management level, Format 66 shows all levels with each goal, objective, strategy, and tactic.

As noted earlier, the purpose of the strategic marketing plan is to determine your next point to obtain and establish the proper courses to permit you to reach that point. In other words, this plan provides you the frame from which to create the numbers; it does not directly create the numbers.

The process of strategic planning for marketing has many parts to make it all work. This plan's role is to get you focused on where you need to be heading. The next step (after the control stage) is to take your strategic marketing plan and convert it into the numbers and actions provided in the marketing plan. The strategy structure you have developed can be turned directly into the marketing plan's activities; in effect, your first marketing plan is your strategic marketing plan with numbers.

The point that needs to be made is that if you desire to have numbers such as sale and revenue forecasts, market structure design (target marketing), cost of marketing, etc., you will need to either go back to your marketing analysis or forward to your marketing plan, pull out the formats provided, and change them to fit the five-year platform.

Format 66

Composite View Summary

	Levels		
	Strategic	**Departmental**	**Functional**
Goals	Expand business.	Expand sales base (offerings).	Expand sales area.
Objectives	Generate additional sales to reach a growth rate of 5% annually.	Increase product sales by 5% to 10% annually.	Increase sales quotas by 10% per year.
Strategies	Form a business relationship with a similar business to produce and sell products internationally.	Develop criteria for selecting which company to approach and align company with.	Add new products to existing product line by acquiring a product using outside means.
Tactics	Develop a joint venture with ABC Co. to market Brand X in Europe by April of next year.	Obtain signed contracts with ABC Co. and set up marketing system to sell version of Brand X.	Enhance the attractiveness of Brand X by lowering the price of our version.

Unit 6

Controlling Your Marketing Strategies

In the strategic marketing plan, you need to design control procedures to monitor the effectiveness of your plan and allow you to make adjustments based on changes in the marketplace. No matter how well planned your marketing strategies are, forces such as marketplace variables, new information, and changing government regulations can require you to alter your plan of action. The process of marketing control begins with establishing marketing management tracking procedures. You will then design checkpoints to adjust your marketing thinking.

ESTABLISHING YOUR CONTROL PROCEDURES

The final component of strategic planning is establishing control over your marketing intentions. You have established your needs, problems, and opportunities; you have determined your mission; you have set your goals and objectives; and you have programmed your strategies, which contain your tactics. At this point, you need to monitor those elements and track how effective you are at performing them. Then you need to design safeguards to try to protect your plan from oversights and market, product, or marketing changes. These safeguards allow you to be aware of what you need to do and give you procedures to follow in altering your plan.

Why Should You Create Controls?

The purpose of control in the marketing environment is to establish set procedures in the event of a product, market, or marketing activity change or misinterpretation. Even though the marketing system in this series has an objective basis, it still comes down to subjectively extracting and interpreting data. As a result, even the most knowledgeable and sensitive marketer can go off track. If you add the fact that so much of marketing is unpredictable and out of control, you will see that you need to design your plan in a way that allows you to see if something is happening differently than you originally thought. Then control procedures will allow you to adjust, stay on course, and obtain your objectives.

How Can You Create Controls?

Control beings with understanding the variables that influence your plans—good or bad and strong or weak. In describing control, you need to establish how you will monitor your plan's progress. You will need to outline those variables you will monitor and by what method you will monitor them. Then you need to put in place a structure that reacts to additional needs, problems, and opportunities that may occur. Control means you are trying to head off a force before it can adversely affect you. Controls also provide you with means to modify your current marketing thinking.

What Are the Elements of Control?

The elements that make up control are monitoring and updating. *Monitoring* basically means a system of evaluating, reporting, and researching events that may be affecting your marketing endeavors. This system must allow you to measure the results on an ongoing basis as well as at the end. *Updating* means taking the information from your monitoring efforts and acting (if needed) to adjust your present marketing actions. The major component here is establishing a contingency plan to your strategic marketing plan, as well as simply preparing for your next planning session.

Monitoring the plan's effectiveness.
The primary tools a marketer has available to monitor the marketing plan's performance are sales reports, marketing and media statements, and on-going marketing audit and research activity results. Several of the tracking techniques will require you to use accounting skills. If you don't possess those skills (most marketers don't), you need to work with your accountant or controller regarding marketing's role in the financial environment of your business.

Updating the plan.
As you track and monitor your marketing management performance, you need to be able to intercept your marketing strategies. This ability will allow you to make adjustments to your plan, alter strategies, and prepare for next year's marketing plan or your next strategic marketing plan.

Timetable.
Although the three marketing management levels are all based on a yearly schedule (over five years), each level's time frame is different. Exhibit 6-1 displays each level's timetable for monitoring and updating.

Exhibit 6-1
Control Timetables for Marketing Management Levels

	Yearly	Quarterly	Monthly	Weekly
Strategic Level	χ— — — — — — χ			
Departmental Level	— — — — — — χ— — — — — — χ			
Functional Level	— — — — — — — — — — — — χ — — — — — χ			

CONTROL PROCEDURES FOR EACH SITUATION LEVEL

Now that you have learned what constitutes control, you are ready to apply that knowledge into three marketing management levels for the strategic marketing plan. Each level will have its own control procedures, just as it had its own mission statement, goals and objectives, and strategies.

Strategic Marketing Management Level Control Procedures

Controls at the strategic marketing management level should reflect your marketing actions at the corporate and/or business unit levels. This means that your control procedures should be geared to that level. The strategic marketing management level control procedures should reflect not only strategic thoughts, but also your overall marketing thoughts. Your control procedures should be specific in origin.

Monitoring the plan's effectiveness.
This component shows you how to oversee your marketing strategies. At this level, you are concerned with monitoring sales, income, and marketing expense reports on a quarterly to yearly basis. These reports are generated by the departmental level for the strategic level. They should be submitted in summary form. Format 67 is a modified income statement that can be used for this summary. Other reports that should be produced are the return on investment and product profitability, which should be reviewed on a yearly basis.

There is no trick to evaluating Format 67; it's merely an exercise of comparison. What you are looking for are any sharp, unpredicted changes up or down in your sales, income, or expenses. Then you should check on these changes and evaluate their possible effect on your marketing thinking and plans.

The impact of research results. There are no set formats for research or the results it produces, because research comes in many different forms and can impact your marketing efforts in diverse ways. The key is to be alert in performing ongoing formal or informal research on your marketing activities. Examine the data collected to see if they support your current marketing actions. If they do not, then you should consider changing your actions to meet what the data have indicated.

Measuring results. The final component to monitoring your plan's effectiveness is installing a system of measuring the results as they become available. Once again, there is really no standard format; however, Format 68 could be used to understand the value of your marketing actions.

In figuring growth rates, you need to be careful in understanding actual growth. The standard method of defining growth is by viewing the growth from time period to time period (i.e., year to year). The problem with this method is if you had an unusually good or bad first time period, your growth rate may not truly represent your actual growth. An example would

---

Format 67

Sales/Income/Expense Reports for Strategic Level Control

Item: _____ *Widget* _____   Time Period: _____ *1992* _____

	Dollars	Percentage of Total Sales/Costs
Gross sales		
Product A:	$3,000,000	——
Product B:	1,000,000	——
Total	$4,000,000	——
Less returns/allowances	1,000	——
Net sales	$3,999,000	——
Cost of goods sold	$1,700,000	42.51%
Gross profit	$2,299,000	——
Gross profit margin	57.49	——
Marketing expenses	$800,000	20.01%
General administrative expenses	$500,000	12.50%
Total expenses	$1,300,000	32.51%
Net profit	$999,000	——

---

be if you had negative growth in the first time period and had positive growth in the second time period, your growth rate would on the surface indicate you had a hot growth period. In reality, your growth indicates you are probably breaking even. Another method of figuring growth rates is to establish an industry standard rate. The result is that you can compare your rates with the industry standard rate.

In the format, the rate difference indicates sales growth minus any cost of marketing increases or decreases. The rate should be a plus; if it is not, you have a problem. The rate change at the bottom indicates patterns and trends in the rate difference.

Updating the plan.

Once you have obtained the reports, pored over the information, and verified the results, you will then decide whether and how you need to

---

Format 68

Sales versus Costs Rates for Strategic Level Control

	19 _92_ Rate of Growth (%)	19 _93_ Rate of Growth (%)	19 _94_ Rate of Growth (%)	19 _95_ Rate of Growth (%)	19 _96_ Rate of Growth (%)
Sales growth (by year)	8.0	9.0	12.0	15.0	15.0
Cost of marketing	3.0	5.0	6.0	8.0	8.0
Rate difference	5.0	4.0	6.0	7.0	7.0
Rate change	—	<1.0>	2.0	1.0	0.0

---

adjust your plans. At this level, your changes are like power steering: you don't feel the full effect at first, but slowly your direction does alter. First you determine what adjustments are needed (if any). Then you design alternative avenues or contingency plans. Then you establish a new schedule that reflects your adjustments. Finally, regardless of whether you have changes or not, you need to begin planning and preparing your next strategic marketing plan or your upcoming marketing plan.

Adjustments. Adjustments are slight alterations in your course. Sometimes changes develop with such great power that you are forced to completely change your course, and this is a problem. But assuming changes to your plan are small, your efforts can be summed up as a modification. Adjustments come in many forms and actions: costs, forecasts, objectives, strategies, etc. Format 69 provides you with a place to note your adjustments.

Format 69

Adjustments at the Strategic Level

Activity	Benchmark (Date)
Changes to plan	*1 year—out*
Response to changes	*Within 3 months (1 quarter)*

Contingency plans. Contingency plans mean not only that you have thought about alternative avenues, but also that those plans are ready to go and can be accessed quickly. The purpose of this activity is to provide you with a safety net or even a lifeboat. The point is that you are aware of other courses to exercise that may not be the most desirable, but at least they would still get you where you want to go. Format 70 provides you with a place to record your contingency plans.

Format 70

Contingency Plans at the Strategic Level

Activity	Benchmark (Date)
Possible changes	*Pricing structure*
Alternative strategies	*Lower pricing, lower profits*

Schedule for the next strategic management plan. Regardless of how successful or unsuccessful your planning is, as soon as you put your plan into service, you will need to start the process all over again. The process is initially in the form of preparation and collecting data, but ultimately another time schedule must be configured. In Format 71 you will begin to put into action a timetable where certain activities are gathered.

Format 71

Schedule for the Next Marketing Plan at the Strategic Level

Activity	Time Period: *Year-end*
Updating plans	*Annual*
Additional research	*Annual*
Process preparation	*Annual*

Departmental Marketing Management Level Control Procedures

Controls at the departmental marketing management level should reflect your marketing actions at the department levels. This means that your control procedures should be geared to that level. The departmental marketing management level control procedures should be specific in origin.

Monitoring the plan's effectiveness.
This component shows you how to oversee your marketing strategies. At this level, you are concerned with monitoring the following on a monthly basis: You will use Formats 72–86 in Unit 2 as needed for this component.

- Sales forecast reports (Format 72)

- Revenue projections (Format 73)

- Expense estimates reports (Format 74)

- Market share/size estimates (Format 75)

- Operations trouble-shooter reports (Format 76)

These reports are generated by the departmental level with the help of the individual functional levels. This level is also responsible for providing reports to the strategic level. These reports should be submitted in summary form. The purpose of the reports at this level is to allow you to check on the progress of your forecasts and determine whether they are on track.

Format 77 is a full income statement that you will prepare with the help of an accountant. There is no trick to evaluating this format; it is merely an exercise of comparison. What you are looking for are any sharp, unpredicted changes up or down in your sales, income, or expenses. Then you should check on these changes and evaluate their possible effect on your marketing thinking and plans.

The impact of research results. There are no set formats for research or the results it produces, because research comes in many different forms and can impact your marketing efforts in diverse ways. The key is to be alert in performing ongoing formal or informal research on your marketing activities. Examine the data collected to see if they support your current marketing actions. If they do not, then you should consider changing your actions to meet what the data have indicated.

Measuring results. The final component to monitoring your plan's effectiveness is instituting a system of measuring the results as they become available. Once again, there is really no standard format; however, your goal is to determine the value of your marketing actions.

Updating the plan.
Once you have obtained the reports, pored over the information, and verified the results, you will then decide whether and how you need to adjust your plans. At this level, your changes are a little more noticeable than at the strategic level. First you determine what adjustments are needed (if any). Then you design alternative avenues or contingency plans. Then you establish a new schedule that reflects your adjustments. Finally, regardless of whether you have changes or not, you need to begin planning and preparing your next strategic marketing plan or your upcoming marketing plan.

Adjustments. Adjustments are slight alterations in your course. Sometimes changes develop with such great power that you are forced to completely change your course, and this is a problem. But assuming changes to your plan are small, your efforts can be summed up as a modification. Adjustments come in many forms and actions: costs, forecasts, objectives, strategies, etc. Format 78 provides you with a place to note your adjustments.

Contingency plans. Contingency plans mean not only that you have thought about alternative avenues, but also that those plans are ready to go and can be accessed quickly. The purpose of this activity is to provide you with a safety net or even a lifeboat. The point is that you are aware of other courses to exercise that may not be the most desirable, but at least they would still get you where you want to go. Format 79 provides you with a place to record your contingency plans.

Schedule for the next strategic management plan. Regardless of how successful or unsuccessful your planning is, as soon as you put your plan into service, you will need to start the process all over again. The process is initially in the form of preparation and collecting data, but ultimately another time schedule must be configured. In Format 80 you will begin to put into action a timetable where certain activities are gathered.

Functional Marketing Management Level Control Procedures

Controls at the functional marketing management level should reflect your marketing actions at the functional levels. This means that your control procedures should be geared to that level. Your control procedures should be specific in origin.

Monitoring the plan's effectiveness.
This component shows you how to oversee your marketing strategies. At this level, you are concerned with monitoring the following on a weekly basis:

- Individual function reports:

    - Budget allocation/expenses

    - Project performance

    - Other

- Function reports

    - Marketing research

    - Product management and development

    - Pricing and financial control

- Distribution

- Sales management (selling)

- Advertising

- Promotions

- Public relations

- Legal marketing

These reports are generated by the individual functional areas with the help of the departmental level. This level is also responsible for providing reports to the departmental level for the strategic level. These reports should be submitted in summary form. The purpose of the reports at this level is to allow you to check on the progress of your activities in more detail and determine whether they are on track.

Reporting and evaluating. Each function will have a set format for budgeting, project management, and other activities that may reflect that particular function's value. The reason for this is to establish consistency in preparing information for the upper levels as displayed in those control procedures formats. It is up to you to decide what these formats should look like; however, once again, you could use the marketing analysis or the marketing plan books available in this series to get those formats or format ideas. Format 81 focuses on a salesperson's sales activity. Format 82 considers the order's tie to the advertising medium from which the customer learned about the product. Format 83 focuses on the effectiveness of the medium used. All three are key reports that should be used for evaluation.

The impact of research results. There are no set formats for research or the results it produces, because research comes in many different forms and can impact your marketing efforts in diverse ways. The key is to be alert in performing ongoing formal or informal research on your marketing activities. Examine the data collected to see if they support your current marketing actions. If they do not, then you should consider changing your actions to meet what the data have indicated.

Measuring results. The final component to monitoring your plan's effectiveness is instituting a system of measuring the results as they become available. Once again, there is really no standard format; however, your goal is to determine the value of your marketing actions.

Updating the plan.
Once you have obtained the reports, pored over the information, and verified the results, you will then decide whether and how you need to

adjust your plans. At this level, your changes are very noticeable. Just about any adjustment you make to your function's activities will create immediate impact. First you determine what adjustments are needed (if any). Then you design alternative avenues or contingency plans. Then you establish a new schedule that reflects your adjustments. Finally, regardless of whether you have changes or not, you need to begin planning and preparing your next strategic marketing plan or your upcoming marketing plan.

Adjustments. Adjustments are slight alterations in your course. Sometimes changes develop with such great power that you are forced to completely change your course, and this is a problem. But assuming changes to your plan are small, your efforts can be summed up as a modification. Adjustments come in many forms and actions: costs, forecasts, objectives, strategies, etc. Format 84 provides you with a place to note your adjustments.

Contingency plans. Contingency plans mean not only that you have thought about alternative avenues, but also that those plans are ready to go and can be accessed quickly. The purpose of this activity is to provide you with a safety net or even a lifeboat. The point is that you are aware of other courses to exercise that may not be the most desirable, but at least they would still get you where you want to go. Format 85 provides you with a place to record your contingency plans.

Schedule for the next strategic management plan. Regardless of how successful or unsuccessful your planning is, as soon as you put your plan into service, you will need to start the process all over again. The process is initially in the form of preparation and collecting data, but ultimately another time schedule must be configured. In Format 86 you will begin to put into action a timetable where certain activities are gathered.

Unit 7

Support Material System

With every document you prepare, you should include only the pertinent information; if you were to include every single piece of data, your document would be so full of information that it would be difficult to read and understand. As a result, support material must be prepared to verify your findings.

PREPARING THE EXHIBITS

The preparation needed to develop the exhibits begins with collecting the sources of information you are using, organizing the contacts you have made in collecting that information, and describing how the results of the information were produced. Then you need to make available examples of the data you obtained and used, such as an actual research report you might have accessed. Finally, you must provide any methodologies you used to produce the data estimates.

This activity will provide the reader of the document with hard data in a convenient format. Your objective is to provide the following information:

1. Information source

2. Contacts (names, addresses, and phone numbers)

3. Information obtained (results)

4. Examples (actual raw data)

5. Methodologies (processes used and models or formulas)

Part 2

Data Reporting: Formats

Preparing Your Strategic Marketing Plan

Formats 1 and 2 should be used to help you establish your current marketing situation. See Unit 1 in Part 1 for explanations and examples of the formats.

Format 1

Quantitative View of Marketing Goals and Objectives

Marketing Activity	Goals and Objectives	Time Period

Sales/revenue (volume)

    Individual products

    Product line

Market share (new/repeat customers)

    Holding

    Gaining

Profitability

    Price

    Profit margin

    Return on investment

Marketing costs

    Control

    Percentage of sales

Format 2

Strategic Marketing Formulation

Mission Statement:

Goals:

Objectives:

Strategies:

80

Identifying Your Needs, Problems, and Opportunities

Formats 3-28 should be used to help you assess your marketing needs, problems, and opportunities. See Unit 2 in Part 1 for explanations and examples of the formats.

Format 3

Origin of Market Needs

Need Type	Basis of Need			
	Customer	Competition	Regulatory/Environmental	Other

Format 4

Strength of Market Needs

Need Type and Cause	How long has it existed?	How strong is it?	How valuable is it?	What is its impact?

Format 5

Origin of Product Market Needs

Need Type	Basis of Need		
	Product Feature	Product Benefit	Other

Format 6

Strength of Product Needs

Need Type and Cause	How long has it existed?	How strong is it?	How valuable is it?	What is its impact?

Format 7

Origin of Marketing Activities Needs

	Basis of Need			
Need Type	External	Internal	Other	Marketing Operations

Format 8

Strength of Marketing Activities Needs

Need Type and Cause	How long has it existed?	How strong is it?	How valuable is it?	What is its impact?

Format 9

Origin of Market Problems

Problem Type	Basis of Problem			
	Customer	Competition	Regulatory/Environmental	Other

Format 10

Strength of Market Problems

Problem Type and Cause	How long has it existed?	How strong is it?	How valuable is it?	What is its impact?

Format 11

Origin of Product Problems

Problem Type	Basis of Problem		
	Product Feature	Product Benefit	Other

Format 12

Strength of Product Problems

Problem Type and Cause	How long has it existed?	How strong is it?	How valuable is it?	What is its impact?

Format 13

Origin of Marketing Activities Problems

Problem Type	Basis of Problem			
	External	Internal	Other	Marketing Operations

Format 14

Strength of Marketing Activities Problems

Problem Type and Cause	How long has it existed?	How strong is it?	How valuable is it?	What is its impact?

Format 15

Origin of Market Opportunities

	Basis of Opportunities			
Opportunity Type	Customer	Competition	Regulatory/Environmental	Other

Format 16

Strength of Market Opportunities

Opportunity Type and Cause	How long has it existed?	How strong is it?	How valuable is it?	What is its impact?

Format 17

Origin of Product Opportunities

Opportunity Type	Basis of Opportunity		
	Product Feature	Product Benefit	Other

Format 18

Strength of Product Opportunities

Opportunity Type and Cause	How long has it existed?	How strong is it?	How valuable is it?	What is its impact?

Format 19

Origin of Marketing Activities Opportunities

Opportunity Type	Basis of Opportunity			
	External	Internal	Other	Marketing Operations

Format 20

Strength of Marketing Activities Opportunities

Opportunity Type and Cause	How long has it existed?	How strong is it?	How valuable is it?	What is its impact?

Format 21

Marketplace Assessment

Importance (#)   Origins

Need:

Problem:

Opportunity:

Strengths

Need:

Problem:

Opportunity:

Format 22

Product Offerings Assessment

Importance (#)	Origins

Need:

Problem:

Opportunity:

	Strengths

Need:

Problem:

Opportunity:

Format 23

Marketing Activities Assessment

Importance (#)   Origins

Need:

Problem:

Opportunity:

Strengths

Need:

Problem:

Opportunity:

Format 24

Final Conclusions Assessment

	Origins		
Importance	**(#) 1**	**(#) 2**	**(#) 3**
Need:			
Situation Area:			
Problem:			
Situation Area:			
Opportunity:			
Situation Area:			

Format 25

Ranking or Rating Origin Strengths or Weaknesses

System Used:

	Strengths/Weaknesses									
	1	2	3	4	5	6	7	8	9	10
Need:										
1	1	2	3	4	5	6	7	8	9	10
2	1	2	3	4	5	6	7	8	9	10
3	1	2	3	4	5	6	7	8	9	10
Problem:										
1	1	2	3	4	5	6	7	8	9	10
2	1	2	3	4	5	6	7	8	9	10
3	1	2	3	4	5	6	7	8	9	10
Opportunity:										
1	1	2	3	4	5	6	7	8	9	10
2	1	2	3	4	5	6	7	8	9	10
3	1	2	3	4	5	6	7	8	9	10

Format 26

Marketing Direction

Action:	Change (-) Decrease	No Change (0) Maintain	Change (+) Increase	Results (Sample)Total
Marketing Research	10-1	0	1-10	
Product Management	10-1	0	1-10	
Pricing	10-1	0	1-10	
Distribution	10-1	0	1-10	
Sales Management	10-1	0	1-10	
Advertising	10-1	0	1-10	
Promotions	10-1	0	1-10	
Public Relations	10-1	0	1-10	
Legal Activities	10-1	0	1-10	
Operational Duties	10-1	0	1-10	

TOTAL

Format 27

Needs, Problems, and Opportunities Summary

Importance (#)	Levels		
	Marketplace	Product Offerings	Marketing Activities

Strategic:

_____

_____

_____

_____

_____

_____

_____

Departmental:

_____

_____

_____

_____

_____

_____

_____

Functional:

_____

_____

_____

_____

_____

_____

_____

Format 28

Ability to Change Actions

	Limits	Capabilities	Changes
Internal			
External			
Changes			

Formulating Your Mission Statement

Formats 29–34 should be used to help you formulate your mission statement. See Unit 3 in Part 1 for explanations and examples of the formats.

Format 29

Strategic Marketing Management Mission Statement

Variable	Interpretation
Who are you?	
What do you offer?	
Whom do you serve?	
Where will you serve?	

Format 30

Strategic Marketing Management Commitment Level

Variable	Interpretation
Financial Resources	
Human Resources	
Physical Resources	

Format 31

Departmental Marketing Management Mission Statement

Variable	Interpretation
Who are you?	
What do you offer?	
Whom do you serve?	
Where will you serve?	

Format 32

Departmental Marketing Management Commitment Level

Variable	Interpretation
Financial Resources	
Human Resources	
Physical Resources	

Format 33

Functional Marketing Management Mission Statement

Variable	Interpretation
Who are you?	
What do you offer?	
Whom do you serve?	
Where will you serve?	

Format 34

Functional Marketing Management Commitment Level

Variable	Interpretation
Financial Resources	
Human Resources	
Physical Resources	

114

Formulating Your Goals and Objectives

Formats 35–41 should be used to help you formulate your goals and objectives. See Unit 4 in Part 1 for explanations and examples of the formats.

Format 35

Establishing Your Strategic Marketing Management Goals

Variable	Interpretation	Expected Gains
What do you want to obtain?		
When do you want to obtain it?		

Interpretation	Short-Term Time Frame	Long-Term Time Frame

Variable	Interpretation	Expected Gains
What do you want to obtain?		
When do you want to obtain it?		

Interpretation	Short-Term Time Frame	Long-Term Time Frame

Variable	Interpretation	Expected Gains
What do you want to obtain?		
When do you want to obtain it?		

Interpretation	Short-Term Time Frame	Long-Term Time Frame

Variable	Interpretation	Expected Gains
What do you want to obtain?		
When do you want to obtain it?		

Interpretation	Short-Term Time Frame	Long-Term Time Frame

Format 36

Strategic Marketing Management Objectives

Outcome Measurement—Activity

Variable	By _____ % Increase	Time Frame

Achievement Milestones—Indicators

Variable	By _____ % Increase	Milestones

Summary

	Goal	Objective
Need:		
Problem:		
Opportunity:		

Format 37

Establishing Your Departmental Marketing Management Goals

Variable	Interpretation	Expected Gains
What do you want to obtain?		
When do you want to obtain it?		

Interpretation	Short-Term Time Frame	Long-Term Time Frame

Variable	Interpretation	Expected Gains
What do you want to obtain?		
When do you want to obtain it?		

Interpretation	Short-Term Time Frame	Long-Term Time Frame

Variable	Interpretation	Expected Gains
What do you want to obtain?		
When do you want to obtain it?		

Interpretation	Short-Term Time Frame	Long-Term Time Frame

Variable	Interpretation	Expected Gains
What do you want to obtain?		
When do you want to obtain it?		

Interpretation	Short-Term Time Frame	Long-Term Time Frame

Format 38

Departmental Marketing Management Objectives

Outcome Measurement—Activity

Variable	By _____ % Increase	Time Frame

Achievement Milestones—Indicators

Variable	By _____ % Increase	Milestones

Summary

	Goal	Objective
Need:		
Problem:		
Opportunity:		

Format 39

Establishing Your Functional Marketing Management Goals

Variable	Interpretation	Expected Gains
What do you want to obtain?		
When do you want to obtain it?		

Interpretation	Short-Term Time Frame	Long-Term Time Frame

Variable	Interpretation	Expected Gains
What do you want to obtain?		
When do you want to obtain it?		

Interpretation	Short-Term Time Frame	Long-Term Time Frame

Variable	Interpretation	Expected Gains
What do you want to obtain?		
When do you want to obtain it?		

Interpretation	Short-Term Time Frame	Long-Term Time Frame

Variable	Interpretation	Expected Gains
What do you want to obtain?		
When do you want to obtain it?		

Interpretation	Short-Term Time Frame	Long-Term Time Frame

Format 40

Functional Marketing Management Objectives

Outcome Measurement—Activity

Variable	By _____ % Increase	Time Frame

Achievement Milestones—Indicators

Variable	By _____ % Increase	Milestones

Summary

	Goal	Objective
Need:		
Problem:		
Opportunity:		

Format 41

Composite View Summary

	Levels		
	Strategic	**Departmental**	**Functional**
Goal			
Objective			

122

Formulating Your Marketing Strategy

Formats 42-66 should be used to help you formulate your marketing strategy. See Unit 5 in Part 1 for explanations and examples of the formats.

Format 42

Budget Allocation for Strategic Level (Five-Year Time Frame)

Goal/Objective: _____

Variable	Strategy ($)	Tactic ($)	Tactic ($)
Funding Commitment (Cost to Deliver Strategy)			

Goal/Objective: _____

Variable	Strategy ($)	Tactic ($)	Tactic ($)
Funding Commitment (Cost to Deliver Strategy)			

Goal/Objective: _____

Variable	Strategy ($)	Tactic ($)	Tactic ($)
Funding Commitment (Cost to Deliver Strategy)			

Goal/Objective: _____

Variable	Strategy ($)	Tactic ($)	Tactic ($)
Funding Commitment (Cost to Deliver Strategy)			

Goal/Objective: _____

Variable	Strategy ($)	Tactic ($)	Tactic ($)
Funding Commitment (Cost to Deliver Strategy)			

Goal/Objective: _____

Variable	Strategy ($)	Tactic ($)	Tactic ($)
Funding Commitment (Cost to Deliver Strategy)			

Format 43

Activities for Action for Strategic Level

Variable   **Goal/Objective:** _____

Strategy

Tactic

Tactic

Variable   **Goal/Objective:** _____

Strategy

Tactic

Tactic

Variable   **Goal/Objective:** _____

Strategy

Tactic

Tactic

Variable   **Goal/Objective:** _____

Strategy

Tactic

Tactic

Format 44

Project/Task Assigning for Strategic Level

Goal/Objective: _____

Variable	Strategy	Tactic	Tactic
Management/Control			
Reporting			

Goal/Objective: _____

Variable	Strategy	Tactic	Tactic
Management/Control			
Reporting			

Goal/Objective: _____

Variable	Strategy	Tactic	Tactic
Management/Control			
Reporting			

Goal/Objective: _____

Variable	Strategy	Tactic	Tactic
Management/Control			
Reporting			

Goal/Objective: _____

Variable	Strategy	Tactic	Tactic
Management/Control			
Reporting			

Goal/Objective: _____

Variable	Strategy	Tactic	Tactic
Management/Control			
Reporting			

Format 45

Measurement of Performance for Strategic Level

Goal/Objective: _____

Variable	Strategy	Tactic	Tactic
Results Appraisal			
Financial			
Organization			
Product Value/Performance			
Quality Control			
Public Opinion			
Marketing Capabilities			
Market Presence			
Other			

Format 46

Structure Verification for Strategic Level

Goal/Objective: _____

Variable	Budget Allocation	Project/Task Assigning	Measurement of Performance
Point (A):			
Strategy			
Tactic			
Tactic			
Point (B):			

A: Where you are now

B: Where you want to go

Goal/Objective: _____

Variable	Budget Allocation	Project/Task Assigning	Measurement of Performance
Point (A):			
Strategy			
Tactic			
Tactic			
Point (B):			

A: Where you are now

B: Where you want to go

Format 47

Time Frame for Strategic Level

Variable   **Goal and Objectives:** _____

Short-Term Strategies

Strategy #1

Strategy

Long-Term Strategies

Strategy #2

Strategy

Format 48

Project/Task Timetable Coordination for Strategic Level

19 ___

	Jan.	Feb.	March	April	May	June	July	Aug.	Sept.	Oct.	Nov.	Dec.
Strategy #1												
Strategy #2												

Format 48 (Continued)

Project/Task Timetable Coordination for Strategic Level

19 ____

	Jan.	Feb.	March	April	May	June	July	Aug.	Sept.	Oct.	Nov.	Dec.
Strategy #1												
Strategy #2												

Format 48 (Continued)

Project/Task Timetable Coordination for Strategic Level

19 ____

	Jan.	Feb.	March	April	May	June	July	Aug.	Sept.	Oct.	Nov.	Dec.
Strategy #1												
Strategy #2												

Format 48 (Continued)

Project/Task Timetable Coordination for Strategic Level

19 ___

	Jan.	Feb.	March	April	May	June	July	Aug.	Sept.	Oct.	Nov.	Dec.
Strategy #1												
Strategy #2												

Format 48 (Continued)

Project/Task Timetable Coordination for Strategic Level

19 ____

	Jan.	Feb.	March	April	May	June	July	Aug.	Sept.	Oct.	Nov.	Dec.
Strategy #1												
Strategy #2												

Format 49

Benchmark Control for Strategic Level

	Evaluation Point (Date/Time)	Action (Safeguard)	Re-initiate Option
Strategy			
Strategy			

Format 50

Budget Allocation for Departmental Level (Five-Year Time Frame)

Goal/Objective: _____

Variable	Strategy ($)	Tactic ($)	Tactic ($)
Funding Commitment (Cost to Deliver Strategy)			

Goal/Objective: _____

Variable	Strategy ($)	Tactic ($)	Tactic ($)
Funding Commitment (Cost to Deliver Strategy)			

Goal/Objective: _____

Variable	Strategy ($)	Tactic ($)	Tactic ($)
Funding Commitment (Cost to Deliver Strategy)			

Goal/Objective: _____

Variable	Strategy ($)	Tactic ($)	Tactic ($)
Funding Commitment (Cost to Deliver Strategy)			

Goal/Objective: _____

Variable	Strategy ($)	Tactic ($)	Tactic ($)
Funding Commitment (Cost to Deliver Strategy)			

Goal/Objective: _____

Variable	Strategy ($)	Tactic ($)	Tactic ($)
Funding Commitment (Cost to Deliver Strategy)			

Format 51

Activities for Action for Departmental Level

Variable   **Goal/Objective:** _____

Strategy

Tactic

Tactic

Variable   **Goal/Objective:** _____

Strategy

Tactic

Tactic

Variable   **Goal/Objective:** _____

Strategy

Tactic

Tactic

Variable   **Goal/Objective:** _____

Strategy

Tactic

Tactic

Format 52

Project/Task Assigning for Departmental Level

Goal/Objective: _____

Variable	Strategy	Tactic	Tactic
Management Control			
Reporting			

Goal/Objective: _____

Variable	Strategy	Tactic	Tactic
Management Control			
Reporting			

Goal/Objective: _____

Variable	Strategy	Tactic	Tactic
Management Control			
Reporting			

Goal/Objective: _____

Variable	Strategy	Tactic	Tactic
Management Control			
Reporting			

Goal/Objective: _____

Variable	Strategy	Tactic	Tactic
Management Control			
Reporting			

Goal/Objective: _____

Variable	Strategy	Tactic	Tactic
Management Control			
Reporting			

Format 53

Measurement of Performance for Departmental Level

Goal/Objective: _____

Variable	Strategy	Tactic	Tactic
Results Appraisal			
Financial			
Organization			
Product Value/Performance			
Quality Control			
Public Opinion			
Marketing Capabilities			
Market Presence			
Other			

Format 54

Structure Verification for Departmental Level

Goal/Objective: _____

Variable	Budget Allocation	Project/Task Assigning	Measurement of Performance
Point (A):			
Strategy			
Tactic			
Tactic			
Point (B):			

A: Where you are now

B: Where you want to go

Goal/Objective: _____

Variable	Budget Allocation	Project/Task Assigning	Measurement of Performance
Point (A):			
Strategy			
Tactic			
Tactic			
Point (B):			

A: Where you are now

B: Where you want to go

140

Format 55

Time Frame for Departmental Level

Variable   Goal and Objectives: _____

Short-Term Strategies

Strategy #1

Strategy

Long-Term Strategies

Strategy #2

Strategy

Format 56

Project/Task Timetable Coordination for Departmental Level

19 ____

	Jan.	Feb.	March	April	May	June	July	Aug.	Sept.	Oct.	Nov.	Dec.
Strategy #1												
Strategy #2												

Format 56 (Continued)

Project/Task Timetable Coordination for Departmental Level

19 ____

	Jan.	Feb.	March	April	May	June	July	Aug.	Sept.	Oct.	Nov.	Dec.
Strategy #1												
Strategy #2												

Format 56 (Continued)

Project/Task Timetable Coordination for Departmental Level

19 ____

	Jan.	Feb.	March	April	May	June	July	Aug.	Sept.	Oct.	Nov.	Dec.
Strategy #1												
Strategy #2												

Format 56 (Continued)

Project/Task Timetable Coordination for Departmental Level

19 _____

	Jan.	Feb.	March	April	May	June	July	Aug.	Sept.	Oct.	Nov.	Dec.
Strategy #1												
Strategy #2												

Format 56 (Continued)

Project/Task Timetable Coordination for Departmental Level

19 ____

	Jan.	Feb.	March	April	May	June	July	Aug.	Sept.	Oct.	Nov.	Dec.
Strategy #1												
Strategy #2												

Format 57

Benchmark Control for Departmental Level

	Evaluation Point (Date/Time)	Action (Safeguard)	Re-initiate Option
Strategy			
Strategy			

Format 58

Budget Allocation for Functional Level (Five-Year Time Frame)

Goal/Objective: _____

Variable	Strategy ($)	Tactic ($)	Tactic ($)
Funding Commitment (Cost to Deliver Strategy)			

Goal/Objective: _____

Variable	Strategy ($)	Tactic ($)	Tactic ($)
Funding Commitment (Cost to Deliver Strategy)			

Goal/Objective: _____

Variable	Strategy ($)	Tactic ($)	Tactic ($)
Funding Commitment (Cost to Deliver Strategy)			

Goal/Objective: _____

Variable	Strategy ($)	Tactic ($)	Tactic ($)
Funding Commitment (Cost to Deliver Strategy)			

Goal/Objective: _____

Variable	Strategy ($)	Tactic ($)	Tactic ($)
Funding Commitment (Cost to Deliver Strategy)			

Goal/Objective: _____

Variable	Strategy ($)	Tactic ($)	Tactic ($)
Funding Commitment (Cost to Deliver Strategy)			

Format 59

Activities for Action for Functional Level

Variable   **Goal/Objective:** _____

Strategy

Tactic

Tactic

Variable   **Goal/Objective:** _____

Strategy

Tactic

Tactic

Variable   **Goal/Objective:** _____

Strategy

Tactic

Tactic

Variable   **Goal/Objective:** _____

Strategy

Tactic

Tactic

Format 60

Project/Task Assigning for Functional Level

Goal/Objective: _____

Variable	**Strategy**	**Tactic**	**Tactic**
Management/Control			
Reporting			

Goal/Objective: _____

Variable	**Strategy**	**Tactic**	**Tactic**
Management/Control			
Reporting			

Goal/Objective: _____

Variable	**Strategy**	**Tactic**	**Tactic**
Management/Control			
Reporting			

Goal/Objective: _____

Variable	**Strategy**	**Tactic**	**Tactic**
Management/Control			
Reporting			

Goal/Objective: _____

Variable	**Strategy**	**Tactic**	**Tactic**
Management/Control			
Reporting			

Goal/Objective: _____

Variable	**Strategy**	**Tactic**	**Tactic**
Management/Control			
Reporting			

Format 61

Measurement of Performance for Functional Level

Goal/Objective: _____

Variable	Strategy	Tactic	Tactic
Results Appraisal			
Financial			
Organization			
Product Value/Performance			
Quality Control			
Public Opinion			
Marketing Capabilities			
Market Presence			
Other			

Format 62

Structure Verification for Functional Level

Goal/Objective: _____

Variable	Budget Allocation	Project/Task Assigning	Measurement of Performance
Point (A):			
Strategy			
Tactic			
Tactic			
Point (B):			

A: Where you are now

B: Where you want to go

Goal/Objective: _____

Variable	Budget Allocation	Project/Task Assigning	Measurement of Performance
Point (A):			
Strategy			
Tactic			
Tactic			
Point (B):			

A: Where you are now

B: Where you want to go

Format 63

Time Frame for Functional Level

Variable	Goal and Objectives: _____
Short-Term Strategies	
Strategy #1	
Strategy	
Long-Term Strategies	
Strategy #2	
Strategy	

Format 64

Project/Task Timetable Coordination for Functional Level

19 ___

	Jan.	Feb.	March	April	May	June	July	Aug.	Sept.	Oct.	Nov.	Dec.
Strategy #1												
Strategy #2												

Format 64 (Continued)

Project/Task Timetable Coordination for Functional Level

19 ____

	Jan.	Feb.	March	April	May	June	July	Aug.	Sept.	Oct.	Nov.	Dec.
Strategy #1												
Strategy #2												

Format 64 (Continued)

Project/Task Timetable Coordination for Functional Level

19 ____

	Jan.	Feb.	March	April	May	June	July	Aug.	Sept.	Oct.	Nov.	Dec.
Strategy #1												
Strategy #2												

Format 64 (Continued)

Project/Task Timetable Coordination for Functional Level

19 ____

	Jan.	Feb.	March	April	May	June	July	Aug.	Sept.	Oct.	Nov.	Dec.
Strategy #1												
Strategy #2												

Format 64 (Continued)

Project/Task Timetable Coordination for Functional Level

19 ___

	Jan.	Feb.	March	April	May	June	July	Aug.	Sept.	Oct.	Nov.	Dec.
Strategy #1												
Strategy #2												

Format 65

Benchmark Control for Strategic Level

	Evaluation Point (Date/Time)	Action (Safeguard)	Re-initiate Option
Strategy			
Strategy			

Format 65

Format 66

Composite View Summary

	Levels		
	Strategic	Departmental	Functional
Goals			
Objectives			
Strategies			
Tactics			

Controlling Your Marketing Strategies

Formats 67–86 should be used to help you monitor and adjust your marketing strategies. See Unit 6 in Part 1 for explanations and examples of the formats.

Format 67

Sales/Income/Expense Reports for Strategic Level Control

Item: _____   Time Period: _____

	Dollars	Percentage of Total Sales/Costs
Gross sales		
Product A:		
Product B:		
Total		
Less returns/allowances		
Net sales		
Cost of goods sold		
Gross profit		
Gross profit margin		
Marketing expenses		
General administrative expenses		
Total expenses		
Net profit		

Format 68

Sales versus Costs Rates for Strategic Level Control

	19 ___ Rate of Growth (%)	19 ___ Rate of Growth (%)	19 ___ Rate of Growth (%)	19 ___ Rate of Growth (%)	19 ___ Rate of Growth (%)
Sales growth (by year)					
Cost of marketing					
Rate difference					
Rate change					

Format 69

Adjustments at the Strategic Level

Activity   **Benchmark (Date)**

Changes to plan

Response to changes

Activity   **Benchmark (Date)**

Changes to plan

Response to changes

Activity   **Benchmark (Date)**

Changes to plan

Response to changes

Activity   **Benchmark (Date)**

Changes to plan

Response to changes

Activity   **Benchmark (Date)**

Changes to plan

Response to changes

Format 70

Contingency Plans at the Strategic Level

Activity   **Benchmark (Date)**

Possible changes

Alternative strategies

Activity   **Benchmark (Date)**

Possible changes

Alternative strategies

Activity   **Benchmark (Date)**

Possible changes

Alternative strategies

Activity   **Benchmark (Date)**

Possible changes

Alternative strategies

Activity   **Benchmark (Date)**

Possible changes

Alternative strategies

Format 71

Schedule for the Next Marketing Plan at the Strategic Level

Activity	Time Period: _____
Updating plans	
Additional research	
Process preparation	

Format 72

Sales Forecast for Departmental Level Control

	Time:		Rate of Growth	Time:		Rate of Growth	Time:		Rate of Growth	Time:		Rate of Growth	Time:		Rate of Growth
	$	Units	(%)	$	Units	(%)	$	Units	(%)	$	Units	(%)	$	Units	(%)
Product:															
Product:															
Product:															
Product:															
Product:															
Product:															
Product:															
Product:															
Product:															
Product:															
Product:															
Product:															
Product:															
Product:															
Product:															
Product:															
Product:															
Product:															
Total															

Format 73

Revenue Projections for Departmental Level Control

Overall Product Line

	Time Period				
	1	**2**	**3**	**4**	**5**
Sales ($)					
Sales (Units)					
Rate of growth (%)					
Cost of goods sold					
Gross profit ($)					
Gross margin (%)					

Individual Product: _____ Time Period

	Time Period				
	1	**2**	**3**	**4**	**5**
Sales ($)					
Sales (Units)					
Rate of growth (%)					
Cost of goods sold					
Gross profit ($)					
Gross margin (%)					

Format 74

Expense Estimates for Departmental Level Control

	Time:		Percentage of Sales	Time:		Percentage of Sales	Time:		Percentage of Sales	Time:		Percentage of Sales	Time:		Percentage of Sales
	$	Units		$	Units		$	Units		$	Units		$	Units	
Marketing research															
Product development															
Pricing															
Distribution															
Sales management															
Advertising															
Promotion															
Public relations															
Legal activities															
Total															
Percentage of sales															
Other marketing expenses															
Total															
Percentage of sales															

Format 75

Market Share/Size for Departmental Level Control

	Time: _____		Rate of Growth	Time: _____		Rate of Growth	Time: _____		Rate of Growth	Time: _____		Rate of Growth	Time: _____		Rate of Growth
	$	Units	(%)	$	Units	(%)	$	Units	(%)	$	Units	(%)	$	Units	(%)

Market Potential

Overall:

Product:

Product:

Market Forecast

Overall:

Product:

Product:

Sales Potential

Overall:

Product:

Product:

Sales Forecast

Overall:

Product:

Product:

Format 75 (Continued)

Market Share/Size for Departmental Level Control

	Time: ——— $ Units	Rate of Growth (%)	Time: ——— $ Units	Rate of Growth (%)	Time: ——— $ Units	Rate of Growth (%)	Time: ——— $ Units	Rate of Growth (%)	Time: ——— $ Units	Rate of Growth (%)
Market Share (Units)										
Market Share (Relative to Market)										
Overall:										
Product:										
Product:										
Market Share (Relative to Competition)										
Overall:										
Product:										
Product:										

Format 76

Operations Trouble-Shooter for Departmental Level Control

	Time Period				
	1	2	3	4	5
Staff status					
Policies/procedures					
MIS					
Internal communications					
Project management					

Format 77

Item: _____   Time Period: _____

	Dollars	Percentage of Total Sales/Costs
Gross sales		
Product A:		
Product B:		
Total		
Less returns/allowances		
Net sales		
Cost of goods sold		
Beginning inventory		
Cost of goods purchased		
Total merchandise handled		
Ending inventory		
Total		
Gross profit		
Gross profit margin		
Marketing expenses		
Marketing functions		
Warehousing		
Regional office expenses		
Total		
General administrative expenses		
Executive salaries		
Clerical expense		
Payroll taxes and insurance		
Office expenses		
Depreciation		
Credit/collections		
Research/development costs		
Other expenses		
Total		
Total Expenses		
Net profit		

Format 78

Adjustments at the Departmental Level

Activity   **Benchmark (Date)**

Changes to plan

Response to changes

Activity   **Benchmark (Date)**

Changes to plan

Response to changes

Activity   **Benchmark (Date)**

Changes to plan

Response to changes

Activity   **Benchmark (Date)**

Changes to plan

Response to changes

Activity   **Benchmark (Date)**

Changes to plan

Response to changes

Format 79

Contingency Plans at the Departmental Level

Activity   **Benchmark (Date)**

Possible changes

Alternative strategies

Activity   **Benchmark (Date)**

Possible changes

Alternative strategies

Activity   **Benchmark (Date)**

Possible changes

Alternative strategies

Activity   **Benchmark (Date)**

Possible changes

Alternative strategies

Activity   **Benchmark (Date)**

Possible changes

Alternative strategies

Format 80

Schedule for the Next Marketing Plan at the Departmental Level

Activity   **Time Period:** _____

Updating plans

Additional research

Process preparation

Format 81

Sales Report for Functional Level Control

Time Period: _____

Salesperson	Product A	B	C	D	Total

Format 82

Order Processing Tracking for Functional Level Control

Time Period: _____

			Product		
Order Number	A	B	C	D	Total

Format 83

Medium Effectiveness for Functional Level Control

Time Period: _____

Media Selection Sales	Rating	Reach	Frequency

Format 84

Adjustments at the Functional Level

Activity   **Benchmark (Date)**

Changes to plan

Response to changes

Activity   **Benchmark (Date)**

Changes to plan

Response to changes

Activity   **Benchmark (Date)**

Changes to plan

Response to changes

Activity   **Benchmark (Date)**

Changes to plan

Response to changes

Activity   **Benchmark (Date)**

Changes to plan

Response to changes

Format 85

Contingency Plans at the Functional Level

Activity   **Benchmark (Date)**

Possible changes

Alternative strategies

Activity   **Benchmark (Date)**

Possible changes

Alternative strategies

Activity   **Benchmark (Date)**

Possible changes

Alternative strategies

Activity   **Benchmark (Date)**

Possible changes

Alternative strategies

Activity   **Benchmark (Date)**

Possible changes

Alternative strategies

Format 86

Schedule for the Next Marketing Plan at the Functional Level

Activity   **Time Period:** _____

Updating plans

Additional research

Process preparation